PORT-ROYAL HABITATION

The Story of the French and Mi'kmaq at Port-Royal

1604–1613

W. P. Kerr

NIMBUS
PUBLISHING LTD

Dedication

This book is dedicated to my dear friend and mentor, Jim How.
Thank you for the guidance and inspiration.

Copyright © W. P. Kerr, 2005

All rights reserved. No part of this book may be reproduced, stored in a retrieval system or transmitted in any form or by any means without the prior written permission from the publisher, or, in the case of photocopying or other reprographic copying, permission from Access Copyright, 1 Yonge Street, Suite 1900, Toronto, Ontario M5E 1E5.

Nimbus Publishing Limited
PO Box 9166
Halifax, NS   B3K 5M8
(902) 455-4286

Printed and bound in Canada

Design: Kathy Kaulbach, Paragon Design Gorup

Library and Archives Canada Cataloguing in Publication

      Kerr, W. P., 1954-
      Port-Royal Habitation : the story of the French and
      Mi'kmaq at Port-Royal (1604-1613) / W.P. Kerr.
      Includes bibliographical references and index.
      ISBN 1-55109-525-4

1. Port Royal Habitation (N.S.)—History. 2. Micmac Indians—History—17th century.
3. Acadia—History—17th century. 4. Nova Scotia—History—To 1784. 5. Canada—History—To 1663 (New France) I. Title.

FC2043.K47 2005   971.6'01   C2005-901058-4

Canada   The Canada Council | Le Conseil des Arts
         for the Arts | du Canada

We acknowledge the financial support of the Government of Canada through the Book Publishing Industry Development Program (BPIDP) and the Canada Council for our publishing activities.

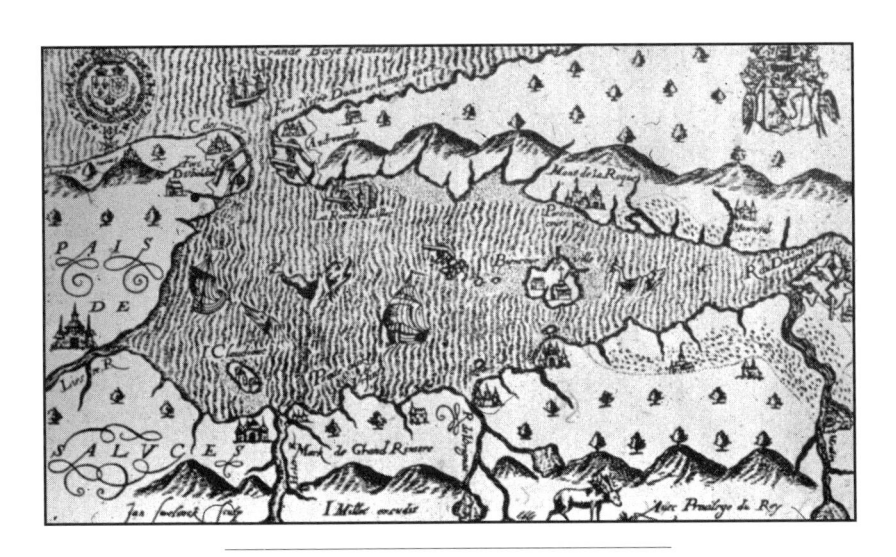

Marc Lescarbot's map (1609) showing a fanciful Port-Royal, with its château-style buildings.

Table of Contents

Acknowledgements vi
Introduction 1

CHAPTER 1   *Quest for Wealth and Territory* 5
Trade Monopolies and Overseas Ambitions 6
De Mons' Grand Scheme 8
Bound for Acadie 12
Our Home is This Country 13
Strangers Along the Coast 16

CHAPTER 2   *St. Croix Island: A Temporary Stopover* 19
Settling In and Learning 20
Island Prison 26
Searching for a Fitting Location 28

CHAPTER 3   *Port-Royal: A Promising Foothold* 31
Second Beginning 32
District of Kespukwitk 35
Turning a Corner 37
Desperation and Jubilation 40
Routine of Daily Life 45
Muskets, Arrows, and Deaths 49
Bountiful Winter of Cheer 51
Betrayals and Sorrowful Departure 58

CHAPTER 4	*Seigneury of Port-Royal* 63	
	Search for Backers and Deceit 64	
	Poutrincourt Returns to His Manoir 65	
	Clash of Secular and Spiritual Powers 70	
	Trading Post and Mission. 76	
	Conflict on the Continent 80	
EPILOGUE	*Continuing French Presence* 87	
	Creation of a National Historic Site 89	
	History Brought to Life 93	
	Bibliography. 101	
	Image Sources 104	
	Index 105	

Acknowledgements

I would like to thank my colleagues A. J. B. (John) Johnston, Wayne Melanson, Claude DeGrâce, and Alan Melanson for reviewing an initial draft of the text. Their constructive comments greatly helped to move the work forward. A special thanks goes to Don Julien, Executive Director of the Confederacy of Mainland Mi'kmaq, who graciously reviewed an earlier version of the manuscript and provided advice on the history of the Mi'kmaq. My gratitude also goes to Donald Soctomah for his advice on Passamaquoddy place names. I also wish to extend my appreciation to Nimbus Publishing Ltd., in particular Sandra McIntyre for her professionalism and encouragement. Finally, but not least, I want to thank the individuals and institutions who have graciously allowed me to include images from their collections.

Introduction

IF ONE WERE TO JUDGE SOLELY by the image typically presented in academic and popular histories, the only significant events to have occurred at the Port-Royal Habitation were the *Theatre of Neptune*, the Order of Good Cheer, and the "conversion" to Catholicism of Mi'kmaw chief Membertou. Yet, what unfolded at what is now Port-Royal National Historic Site of Canada contributed immeasurably to the development of both modern-day Canada and northeastern North America.

The story of Pierre Dugua, Sieur de Mons' settlement in the area the French called La Cadie (Acadie) is a dramatic tale of social, political, economic, and religious intrigue and strife. The history of the first Port-Royal is one of human tenacity, struggles, successes, failures, and cultural clashes as two different peoples and worldviews encountered each other.

The French at Port-Royal played a central role in making the Atlantic area of northeastern North America better known to Europeans. Samuel de Champlain's precise mapping of the coastline from Cape Breton to the Bay of Fundy and on to Cape Cod set a new standard in cartography. Similarly, the collection of natural and other "curiosities" from this part of the "New World" excited interest when they arrived in France. The knowledge the French gained from their contacts and alliances with the Mi'kmaq and other Amerindians during the lifespan of the Port-Royal Habitation provided important insights for those who later went on to Quebec and farther inland.

The 1605 French settlement at Port-Royal pre-dated the English venture at Jamestown, Virginia, by two years; the founding of Quebec by three; and the arrival of the Pilgrims at Plymouth by fifteen. The histories of these four early European settlements are intertwined with each other and with the Amerindian societies that surrounded them, as Europeans struggled to gain a foothold on the continent.

Port-Royal's story is not as well known as it should be, since its influence continued long after its destruction in 1613—the settlement helped lead to the establishment of a permanent French presence in North America.

In order to avoid the vagueness of the expressions "Indian" and "Native," and because it is more specific than "Aboriginal," the author has used the term "Amerindian." Many of the terminologies referring to the Amerindians in the pages that follow are taken from the writings of the French who were at Port-Royal between 1604 and 1613 (see Bibliography). During the early contact period, for example, the early French referred to the Amerindian societies as follows: Souriquois (Mi'kmaq); Etchemins or Etechemins (includes at least the Wolastoqiyik or Maliseet, Passamaquoddy, and Penobscot); and Armouchiquois, or Almouchiquois (general term designating the various Amerindian peoples along the New England coast, west of the Kennebec River, Maine, to the Cape Cod area of Massachusetts). In the pages that follow, however, the present-day names for the Amerindian societies (e.g., Mi'kmaq) are used, except where the author wishes to establish the historical context or when referring generally to Amerindians, or if the specific Amerindian society cannot be identified.

The word "Mi'kmaw" is used as an adjective or denoting an individual. "Mi'kmaq," used as a noun, refers to more than one Mi'kmaw person or the nation.

For the most part, the spellings of personal names come from the *Dictionary of Canadian Biography (DCB)*. The spellings, however, have not been standardized and so the *DCB*—as with the European sources of the period—often provides two or more variations for the same person. Additionally, the spellings of place names in the primary sources are often inconsistent, frequently within the same work. The author, therefore, has mainly used the French place names as they are spelled on Champlain's maps. Thus, in the following pages, the original source place names appear and are followed by the present-day place names in parentheses; the latter are then used, except where the author wishes to establish the historical context.

In their dealings during the early contact period, the Amerindians and French used a language that is typically referred to as "pidgin Basque." French chronicler Marc Lescarbot noted that the Amerindians, including the Mi'kmaq, trading along the coast of the Gaspé (Quebec) spoke a Basque-Algonquian trade language that was "half Basque." This effectively became the "contact" language that was used in speaking with Europeans. As well, Amerindians, such as the Mi'kmaq, acted as intermediaries and interpreters for the French in their dealings with other Amerindian societies. Some French also learned Amerindian dialects and acted as interpreters.

Fortified port of Havre de Grace
(today's Le Havre), France, late 1500s

CHAPTER 1 *Quest for Wealth and Territory*

EARLY MARCH OF 1604. The fortified port of Havre de Grace, on the English Channel, at the mouth of the great River Seine in northern France. Two ships are about to sail for La Cadie (Acadie). The expedition's leader is Pierre Dugua, Sieur de Mons, a Protestant nobleman-courtier and governor of the town of Pons: a position he received from King Henri IV of France and Navarre for his unwavering support during the Wars of Religion in France from 1562 to 1598.

A number of notable gentlemen will accompany Sieur de Mons on the flagship *Don-de-Dieu*: Samuel de Champlain, whom the king has instructed to report on his findings, although he has no official title; Jean Biencourt de Poutrincourt et de Saint-Just, an influential nobleman and de Mons' former comrade-in-arms; and Jean Ralleau (or

Ralluau), personal secretary to de Mons. François Gravé Du Pont, naval captain and merchant, will oversee the second ship, the *Bonne Renommée*.

The Sieur de Mons' roughly 120-person expedition is made up of an eclectic group of characters, which includes the Sieurs du Boulay, d'Orville, de Beaumont, Champdoré *dit* Angibault, Fougeray de Vitré, La Motte Bourgjoli, Genestou, and Sourin; surgeon Philippe Raybois, apothecary Henri Beaufort, two Catholic priests, one a Nicolas Aubry, and an unnamed Protestant pastor, Guillaume Foulques (a spare captain), pilots Guillaume Du Glas, Pierre Cramolet, and Louis Coman, miner Maître Simon; as well as joiners, wood-sawyers, stonecutters, carpenters, blacksmiths, bakers, and a contingent of Swiss mercenaries.

Captains Timothée and Morel shout out orders as their crews load a year's worth of supplies onto the ships: food, weapons, tools, parts for a pinnace, barrels of drinking water, casks of wine, and the crucial European trade goods, including glass beads, rosaries, mirrors, knives, hatchets, iron arrow-points, awls, copper kettles, blankets, and cloaks.

Even though some of the men have been to Canada (Quebec), anticipation still fills the air. In our age of instant satellite communications, it is difficult to imagine what it must have been like for people in the early 1600s to set off for a place that many still considered an exotic land beyond the sea. So what inspired this expedition? Why were they risking their lives in the weeks and months ahead?

Trade Monopolies and Overseas Ambitions

FOR OVER A CENTURY whales and cod had lured Europeans seasonally to northeastern North America, but it was beavers that encouraged them to settle there permanently in the late 1500s.

France joined the competition for overseas expansion later than other Europeans. Portugal and Spain had been profiting from their colonies in Central and South America for years. France's approach changed in 1524, however, when King François I sponsored Italian explorer Giovanni da Verrazzano to explore the North Atlantic coast and to find the supposed route to the Orient. While he did not find the fabled northwest passage, Verrazzano did collect vital information and laid "claim" for France to the eastern coast of North America from the Carolinas to Cape Breton, which he named Nouvelle France.

Gradually, the idea developed to use trade monopolies as a way of

Bust of Pierre Dugua, Sieur de Mons

financing permanent French colonization in order to better control territorial rights and trade, especially in furs. France's treasury was depleted from civil and foreign wars, and so Henri IV's overseas ambitions fell to private interests in exchange for exclusive trade monopolies.

In 1598, the Marquis de La Roche planted a settlement, composed of some forty "vagabonds and beggars" and about ten soldiers, on Sable Island, off the coast of today's Nova Scotia. But five years later the eleven remaining survivors were rescued and taken back to France. In 1600, Pierre de Chauvin, Sieur de Tonnetuit, established a colony at Tadoussac, Quebec, which was abandoned by the following spring (Sieur de Mons and François Gravé Du Pont—hereafter Gravé Du Pont—were members of the expedition). When Chauvin died in early 1603, his grant passed to Commander Aymar de Chaste, who sent three ships to the St. Lawrence

River, one of which, the *Bonne Renommée*, Gravé Du Pont commanded; Champlain also participated.

Then, as Champlain noted, "notwithstanding all these vicissitudes and hesitations, the Sieur de [Mons] desired to attempt this desperate undertaking, and asked his Majesty for a commission for this purpose…"

This time, however, France chose Acadie over the St. Lawrence River for the next attempt at settlement, since, as historian Marcel Trudel writes, "It was here that a site was sought which would combine the ideal conditions for colonization: nearness to the sea, the proximity of peaceable natives, an abundance of mines, a fertile soil, a mild climate, and possible access to the Western sea."

De Mons' Grand Scheme

"Some aim at profit, others at glory, and others at the public welfare. The greater number take to commerce, and especially that which is carried on by sea." Champlain's observation was apt, since it was the potential of huge profits from the fur trade that was the major reason for de Mons' preparations to cross the Atlantic Ocean in 1604.

In the late decades of the 1500s, a new style of headwear had become extremely popular in Europe—the beaver felt hat. Hats made from beaver felt would stay rigid, waterproof, and sturdy in any shape. There were even beaver-felt hats especially designed for children. However, the supply of beaver pelts in Western Europe could not meet the ever-increasing demand and so the French and other Europeans turned to the Amerindians of North America to provide them with a new supply, reasonably cheaply.

The French above all wanted the *castor gras d'hiver* ("greasy winter beaver," commonly called "coat beaver"), when the beaver's natural insulation, the down, was thickest. There were two types of pelts: the ones the Amerindians immediately dried after skinning, and those they had worn. The long guard hairs of the dried pelts, however, had to be combed out in Europe, which increased costs. Consequently, the traders sought especially the Amerindians' cast-off beaver robes, because the more they were worn, the more the long guard hairs of the beaver pelts fell off, leaving the valuable soft under-wool.

There was a downside to the lucrative trade, though not for the traders and furriers, but for the labourers who toiled to make the hats. The

European artist's interpretation of the *Castor canadiensis*

Der Hüter.

Kehrt hie hereyn jr Kauffleut all/
Schauwt/ob mein arbeit euch gefall/
Von guter Wolln/sauber/nicht biltzet/
Wol gschlagen/gwalcken vnd gefiltzet/
Auch wol geformbt vnd zugericht/
Gezogen Hüt vnd auch gebicht/
Auch mach ich der Filtzsocken viel/
Wenn der kalt Winter anbrechn wil.
                                     O   Der

Hatter making a felt hat, around 1570

well-known expression, "mad as a hatter," originates from a felt-making method in which mercury was used. The mercury slowly poisoned the hat-makers, and it was said that some literally went mad!

So the European desire for fashionable apparel gave birth to an empire that was to play a major role in the colonial history of North America.

Sieur de Mons' lobbying paid off on November 8, 1603, when Henri IV issued letters patent appointing him lieutenant general in the "countries, territories, coasts, and confines of La Cadie [Acadie]. To begin from the 40th degree unto the 46th…[from modern-day Philadelphia north to Cape Breton Island and west past Sorel, Quebec, and then as far inland as Sieur de Mons could travel]."[1]

Additionally, the king issued an edict on December 18, banning the trade in furs and other merchandise in "Acadie, Canada (Quebec), and other places in New France," unless the traders held shares in de Mons' company.

The king granted Sieur de Mons near vice-regal powers: he could build forts and settlements, enact laws, wage war, issue land grants and titles, keep most of the profits from all precious metals, and conscript the "vagrant idle person and masterless." In turn, de Mons had to establish sixty colonists a year (reduced from 100), make peace with and convert the Amerindians to Catholicism, and explore and make records of the coast and the presence of precious minerals. To enforce his ten-year monopoly (which was a continuation of the grant of Aymar de Chaste, who had died in September 1603), the Admiral of France appointed de Mons vice-admiral, with the powers to search and seize illegal traders.

By early February 1604, de Mons' company, composed of merchant shareholders from the coastal ports of Rouen, Saint-Malo, La Rochelle, and Saint-Jean-de-Luz, was operational. In addition to the two ships bound for Acadie, the company sent three ships to the St. Lawrence River to trade for furs.

---

[1] Later, Acadie came to typically mean the coastal regions of present-day northern Maine, southern New Brunswick, and all of mainland Nova Scotia.

Bound for Acadie

ON MARCH 7, 1604, Captain Timothée steered the *Don-de-Dieu*, with de Mons and crew, out of Havre de Grace (today's Le Havre). Three days later Captain Morel, Gravé Du Pont, and crew sailed in the *Bonne Renommée*. The plan was for the two ships to rendezvous in Canceau (Canso, Nova Scotia), already a well-known fishing harbour on the coast of Acadie. However, Champlain, writing after the fact, says that "when we were on the high sea, the Sieur de [Mons] changed his mind, and set his course towards Port Mouton, because it is farther south and also a more convenient place to land than Canso."

As his ship neared the coast of Acadie, de Mons likely gave little thought to the impact that his expedition might have on the Amerindians living in this part of northeastern North America. As a typical European businessman of his time, his thoughts were first and foremost on having a successful and profitable voyage.

On this detail of a map (1616) by Samuel de Champlain, the cartographer placed "Acadie" on what is now Maine.

[inset] Type of ship that sailed to Acadie in the early 1600s

Our Home is This Country [2]

THE LAND EUROPEANS VIEWED as a "New World," the many Amerindian societies who lived there saw as their "Ancient Homeland." In their drive for overseas colonies, Europeans, like the Spanish, Portuguese, and French, advanced the interpretation that the continent was a *terra nullius*, a land empty of people, which they used as a legal reason for claiming ownership. Of course they did not find an "untouched wilderness"; yet, as historian Olive Dickason writes: "As they saw it, they also had the right to claim vast stretches of territory that in the European sense were not occupied at all but were 'ranged' rather than settled by their nomadic inhabitants."

Even though French ideas about the Amerindians were still vague, Henri IV knew clearly how "fruitful, opportune, and useful for us" this trade with them could be. Sieur de Mons' expedition would have numerous encounters with Amerindians, yet none was to outlast the relationship that was to develop between the French and the Mi'kmaq—two different worlds were about to meet.

During the early contact period, the people the early French called Souriquois (Mi'kmaq), an Eastern Algonkian-speaking people, appear to have been located throughout present-day Nova Scotia and Prince Edward Island, northeastern New Brunswick, and a part of the Gaspé Peninsula of Quebec. Today's Mi'kmaq call their ancestral homeland Mi'kma'ki.

The Mi'kmaq were chiefly hunters of marine animals before the arrival of Europeans, dependant primarily on marine resources and secondly on those of the forest. Living along the coast in the summer meant that the Mi'kmaq were likely the first Amerindians in northeastern North America to have continual interaction with European explorers and fishermen. This was not surprising given their excellent sailing skills; their ocean-going canoes were ideal for coastal travel, as well as for crossing the Gulf of St. Lawrence and even going to Newfoundland, where European fishermen came each fishing season. They had also adapted themselves to sailing European boats; for example, at Canso in 1606 a French expedition on its way to Port-Royal encountered a shallop with a moose painted on its sail, commanded by Mi'kmaq.

---

[2] A sub-header taken from the book of poems by Mi'kmaw writer Rita Joe, entitled *Poems of Rita Joe*. Halifax: Abenaki Press, 1978.

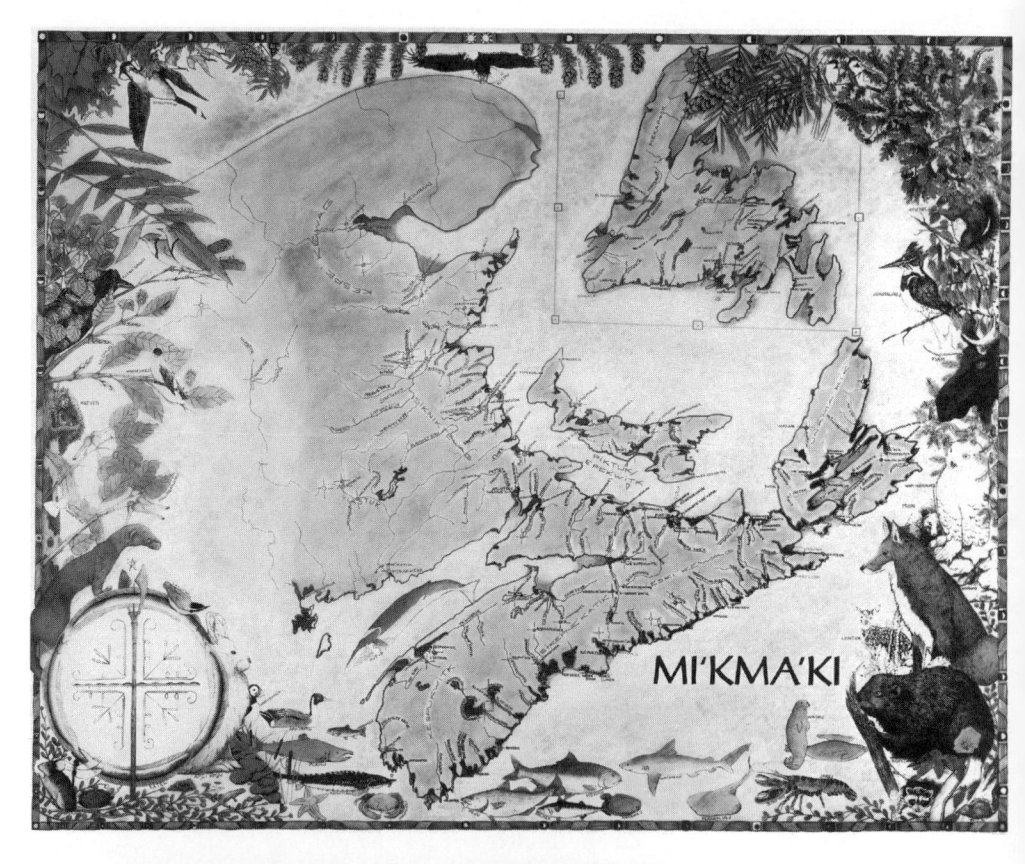

Map of Mi'kma'ki showing the ancient homeland of the Mi'kmaq.

Re-creation of the Mi'kmaq going fishing with spears.

14 ◦ Port-Royal Habitation

Long before the early 1600s, Mi'kmaw and European traders met at established seasonal contact places to trade for furs. These exchanges had prepared the Mi'kmaq for trading relationships with Sieur de Mons. It was not surprising, therefore, that the Mi'kmaq might also become actively involved with permanent European settlements in Mi'kma'ki.

The fur trade in Mi'kma'ki and elsewhere in northeastern North America would have been impossible without the Mi'kmaq and other Amerindians. European traders were simply dependant on the Amerindians' knowledge of the environment, trapping and hunting skills, and trading networks. The Amerindians' early view of the French in their "floating islands" was that they were masters of iron and merchandise, goods the Mi'kmaq and other Amerindians were interested in obtaining. Over time the Mi'kmaq would become middlemen in the barter of furs for European trade goods with other Amerindian societies; in fact the Mi'kmaq were referred to by some as "Taranteens," which apparently meant "traders."

By the late 1500s, however, the fur trade went from being merely a supplementary activity to an extremely competitive business. It was to unleash new economic and cultural forces, forces that were to upset the traditional stability of Mi'kmaw life (and that of other Amerindian societies) in the process.

Watercolour of a Mi'kmaw canoe by W. G. R. Hind, late 1800s

Strangers Along the Coast

AFTER TWO LONG MONTHS AT SEA, and at least one death, Sieur de Mons and crew finally reached Acadie on May 8, at Cap de la Héue (Cape LaHave, Nova Scotia).

The expedition anchored in nearby Port de La heue (Green Bay), where they likely went ashore for fresh water and game and to meet the local Mi'kmaq, whose chief was called Messamouet. Soon after, de Mons' men seized a ship, the *Levrette*, and its cargo, which was trading illegally. They named the place por[t] du Rossÿnol (or Rossignol; today's Liverpool Bay), after the ship's captain. The expedition made its way to nearby port au mouton (Port Mouton), named for the sheep that "leaped overboard and drowned himself, came aboard again, and was taken and eaten as good prize." They stayed roughly three weeks, where "they cabined and lodged

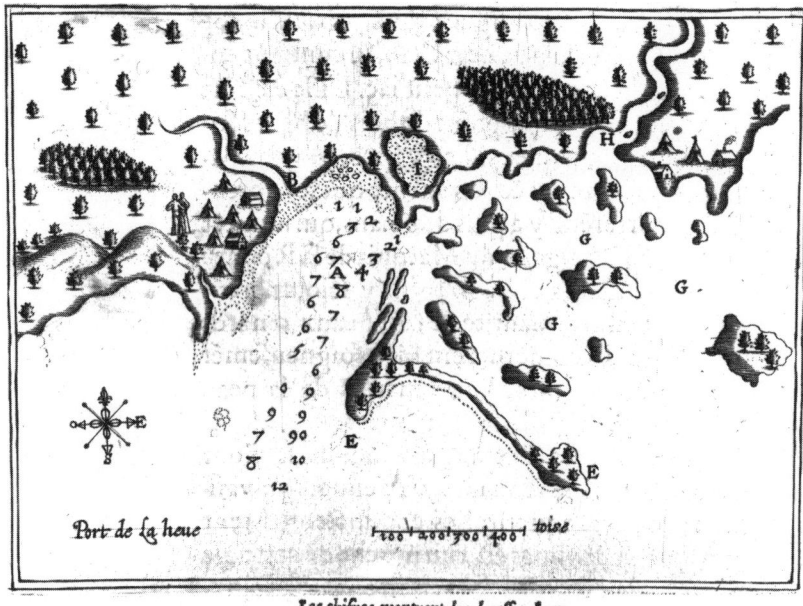

Les chifres montrent les brasses d'eau.

A   Le lieu ou les vaisseaux moullent l'ancre.
B   Vne petite riuiere qui asseche de basse mer.
C   Les lieux ou les sauuages cabannent.
D   Vne basse a l'entree du port
E   Vne petite isle couuerte de bois.
F   Le Cap de la Héue.
G   Vne baye ou il y a quantité d'isles couuertes de bois.
H   Vne riuiere qui va dans les terres 6, ou 7. lieux. auec peu d'eau.
I   Vn estang proche de la mer.

Champlain's map of Port de La heue (Green Bay, and Cape LaHave, Nova Scotia); note the Mi'kmaw wigwams.

themselves after the [Amerindian] fashion," waiting for Gravé Du Pont to arrive, on whose ship were most of the supplies for the coming winter. Meanwhile, Champlain, Jean Ralleau, and ten men set out to explore the coast.

With still no sign of Gravé Du Pont, Sieur de Mons sent one of his men and several Amerindians, probably Mi'kmaq, up the coast towards Canso. The messengers soon found Gravé Du Pont at "La Baie des Iles" (near today's Sheet Harbour, Nova Scotia). He handed over most of the supplies before heading back to Canso to trade for furs. When Champlain and Ralleau returned, the expedition sailed to baye saincte Marie (St. Mary's Bay) where they left the larger vessels while de Mons, Champlain, and Poutrincourt explored the unfamiliar waters in a smaller boat.

They entered an expansive basin, which Champlain named—Lescarbot said it was de Mons—port Royal (Port-Royal, now the Annapolis Basin), because it "is one of the finest harbours I had seen on all these coasts where a couple of thousand vessels could lie in safety." Poutrincourt expressed an interest in the place, which Sieur de Mons subsequently granted to him. For the moment, however, Port-Royal was passed over as a site for settlement. As we shall see, this was de Mons' first serious error.

From Port-Royal they explored the baye Françoise (Bay of Fundy)—so named by de Mons—counter-clockwise, and on June 24, the expedition entered a large river (called Oigoudi by the Etchemins-Wolastoqiyik), which they named R. St Iehan (St. John River) in honour of Saint John the Baptist, whose feast day it was on the Roman Catholic calendar. Continuing westward they entered present-day Passamaquoddy Bay and then sailed up the Riuiere des Etechemins (St. Croix River, now part of the Canada-U.S border; today's Passamaquoddy call it Skutik, pronounced Schoodic, meaning "river by the burnt over land"). The expedition stopped at an island in mid-river, which they "considered the best we had seen, both on account of its situation, the fine country, and for the interaction we were expecting with the [Amerindians] of these coasts and of the interior, since we should be in their midst." De Mons named it Isle de sainte Croix (St. Croix Island) for the intersection of the tributaries above the island, which appeared to form a cross. The Passamaquoddy call the island Mehtonuwekoss, meaning "little out of food place." But as we shall see, this was to be a second and more serious error. To appreciate what unfolded later at Port-Royal, one must first understand what happened during the winter of 1604–05.

Aerial view of modern-day St. Croix Island, with Canadian shoreline in background

CHAPTER 2 *St Croix: A Temporary Stopover*

DEFENCE AGAINST EUROPEAN raids and insecurities about Amerindians were why Sieur de Mons chose St. Croix Island as the initial place for settlement. It was common among European colonists to choose islands, as they were fairly easy to defend. As Champlain wrote, St. Croix Island was "naturally well situated…and is easy to fortify. The shores of the mainland are distant on both sides some nine hundred to a thousand paces, so that vessels could only pass along the river at the mercy of the [cannons, which have a commanding view down river.]"

Passamaquoddy catch sight of the arrival of Sieur de Mons' expedition in 1604

Settling In and Learning

Even though European explorers and fishermen sailed along the northeast coast throughout the 1500s, few seem to have entered Passamaquoddy Bay (which the Passamaquoddy people call Peskotmuhkatik, meaning "place of the pollack spearing people"). The arrival of Sieur de Mons' expedition was likely one of the earliest encounters that the Etchemins (Passamaquoddy) of this area had with Europeans. Yet, while the Passamaquoddy openly greeted these "strangers," the French maintained "a continual watch...by night fearing some surprise from [the Amerindians, presumably Passamaquoddy] that had lodged themselves at the foot of [St. Croix Island,] or some other enemy."

Once the defences were in place, de Mons sent Pierre Champdoré and a small crew to tell the men on the two ships still at St. Mary's Bay to come

Sieur de Mons' men building defences on St. Croix Island

French constructing their settlement on St. Croix Island

ST. CROIX: A TEMPORARY STOPOVER ~ 21

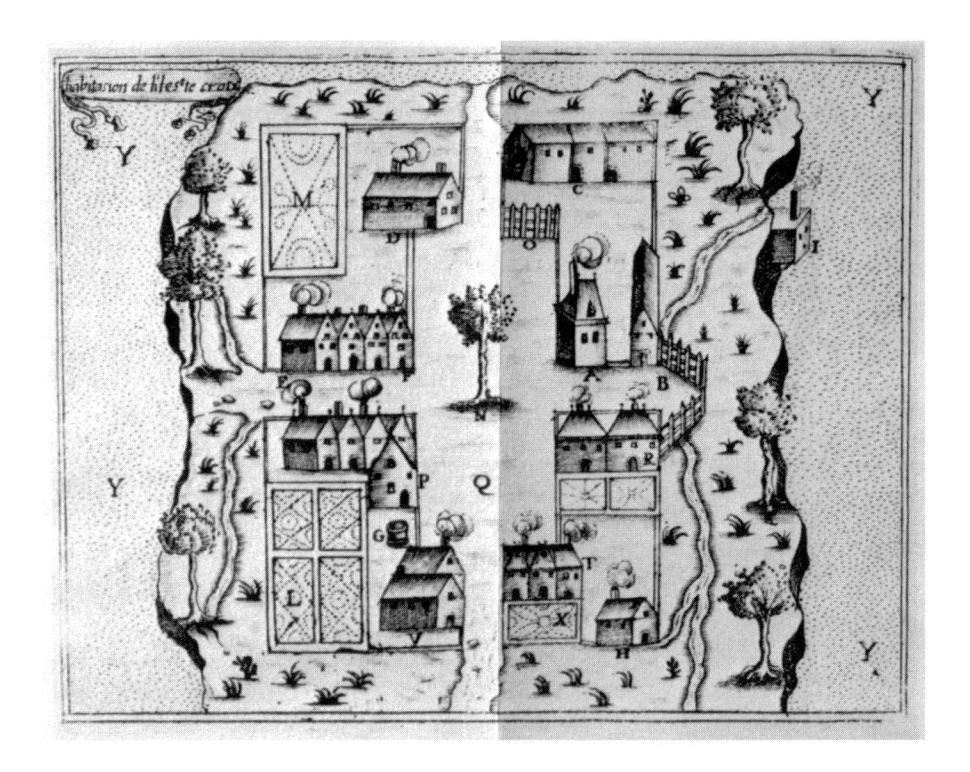

Copperplate engraving likely based on a rough, yet approximately accurate, drawing by Champlain of the St. Croix Island Habitation

MODERN LEGEND
(A) Sieur de Mons' dwelling; (B) Public building when it rained; (C) Storehouse; (D) Quarters for the Swiss; (E) Blacksmith; (F) Carpenters' dwelling; (G) Well; (H) Bake house for making bread; (I) Cook-house; (L) Gardens; (M) Other gardens; (N) Public square with tree in centre; (O) Palisade; (P) Dwellings of Sieurs d'Orville, Champlain & Chandore (Champdoré); (Q) Dwellings of Sieur du Boulay & other workmen; (R) Dwellings of Sieurs de Genestou, Sourin & other workmen; (T) Dwellings of Sieurs de Beaumont, la Motte Bourioli & Fougeray; (V) Our priest's quarters; (X) Other gardens; (Y) River surrounding the island.

to St. Croix Island; they arrived several days later. Champdoré and crew remained in the area to fish and when they reached isle Longue (Long Island), they suddenly spotted a figure on the distant shore waving a hat and handkerchief at the end of a pole. They were astonished to discover that it was the Catholic priest, Nicolas Aubry, who had been given up for dead. Around June 16, while the ships were still at St. Mary's Bay, Aubry misplaced his sword while out for a walk in the woods with several others. He left the group to go and find it, but became lost, and despite the efforts of the French and Mi'kmaq, they could not locate him. He had survived for seventeen days by eating sorrel (a type of herb) and some berries.

Back at St. Croix Island, meanwhile, the Sieur de Mons moved quickly to establish the settlement. He chose the site for the large storehouse, decided upon the plan for his own dwelling, and assigned living places. Then, based on a plan drawn up by Champlain, "all set to work to clear the island, to fetch wood, to cut timber, to carry earth, and other things necessary for the construction…" of what they called their Habitation. All the while, the French newcomers had to fight off hordes of black flies, which bit some so severely that they could hardly see.

The men erected the structures from timbers cut down on the island (and possibly the mainland), excepting de Mons' residence and the large storehouse, which may have been assembled from building frames brought from France. (Lescarbot suggests, unconfirmed by Champlain, that a few may have also housed themselves on the mainland.) They also built a small chapel in the "Indian fashion" at the tip of the island.

They set up a hand-mill for grinding wheat and an oven for baking bread, and established a water-mill and a pit for making charcoal for the forge on the present-day American mainland. Gardens were planted on both the island and the mainland, on both sides of the river. While those on the island wilted in the sandy soil, the ones on the mainland produced bountiful crops of wheat, rye, and vegetables.

Sieur de Mons decided to send Captain Foulques in Rossignol's ship, the *Levrette*, to retrieve the remaining supplies from Gravé Du Pont at Canso. Shortly after his departure, however, Guillaume Du Glas, the pilot of the *Bonne Renommée*, arrived from Canso with two Basque captains whom they had caught fur trading illegally. De Mons treated them kindly, but instructed Du Glas to return them to Gravé Du Pont so he could take them to France to face justice.

Work on the buildings progressed steadily, with "the carpenters at the storehouse and dwelling of the Sieur de [Mons], and all the others [worked on their dwellings]." Champlain worked on his home, which he built with help from his and the Sieur d'Orville's servants.

While in Canada (Quebec) in 1603, Champlain had met merchant Jean Sarcel, Sieur de Prévert, who had apparently told him that there were rich veins of copper at the head of the Bay of Fundy. Thus, with the dreams of finding precious metals, de Mons sent Champlain to search for the supposed copper mine. Nine sailors and Mi'kmaw chief Messamouet (whom the French had likely met earlier at Port de La Heue [Green Bay]), who claimed to know the location of the mine, went with Champlain. Near the St. John River, the group found a small but good deposit of copper and several others of lesser quality, but they were unable to locate the purported rich copper mine and so they returned to St. Croix Island. To his apparent annoyance, Champlain would later discover that Prévert had provided a second-hand account about the mines.

Passamaquoddy, as well as the Mi'kmaq and Wolastoqiyik, acted as guides for the French, and as go-betweens with other Amerindians, along the coast of today's New England.

With the summer waning, de Mons decided to send the ships *Don-de-Dieu* and *Levrette* (the latter to be captained by Foulques, who had returned from Canso) back to France. Also returning were Poutrincourt, Ralleau, so that he could attend to company matters on de Mons' behalf, and the priest Nicolas Aubry, who was still recovering from his ordeal at St. Mary's Bay. In addition, de Mons sent a caribou as a gift for the king. Remarkably, it would survive the voyage but died later of neglect.

The voyage back to France was filled with storms and perils. Once on the high seas, the ship *Don-de-Dieu*, commanded by Captain Timothée, was literally rolled over by a fierce squall "in such a manner that of the one part of the keel was on the face of the water, and the sail swimming upon it...." Pandemonium ensued as the men scrambled to save themselves from drowning. But just when it seemed hopeless, the sail was shredded to pieces and "the ship [then] began to stir and rise again by little and little [and]…the ballast which remained beneath did help to stir her upright." Then a sailor's love of wine prevented yet another near disaster. In the dead of night, a crewman snuck below deck to fill his bottle with wine. But instead of getting his taste of wine he discovered the ship's hold was half-filled with water, "in such sort that the peril was imminent, and they had infinite pains to staunch her by pumping. In the end…they found a great leak by the keel, which they stopped with diligence." Both ships eventually reached France safely.

Back at St. Croix Island, meanwhile, Sieur de Mons had sent Champlain, along with a dozen sailors and two Amerindians (likely Passamaquoddy) acting as guides, on an excursion along the coast of what is now Maine in search of a more suitable place to settle, for de Mons considered the island but a short-term stopover. The expedition soon sighted a large island, transected by a striking mountain range, which Champlain named Mont-deserts (Mount Desert Island). Local Etchemins (Penobscot) guided them up the nearby river they called Peimtegouet (Penobscot River) for about 30 km inland, where—with the two Amerindian guides acting as intermediaries and interpreters—Champlain had a customary parley and feast with Chiefs Bashabes and Cabahis. The former was head-chief of an "alliance" that stretched into Massachusetts. Chief Bashabes and his companions had their customary pipe-smoking before he began his speech, after which he gave Champlain a gift of venison and waterfowl and Champlain "made them presents of hatchets, rosaries, caps, and knives, and other little knick-knacks. The rest of this day and the following night [the Amerindians] did nothing but dance, sing, and make merry, awaiting the dawn when we bartered a certain number of beaver-skins." This was Champlain's first documented formal encounter with the Etchemins and it established the protocol that he was to use in his future encounters. On their way down river, the French stopped at Chief Cabahis' encampment. He then accompanied the French for a short distance, providing Champlain with important details about a portage route from the Penobscot River to the St. Croix River and one via today's Chaudière River to the St. Lawrence River.

The French continued towards the Riuiere de qui ni be quy (Kennebec River), but without their Amerindian guides because "they were unwilling to come to Kennebec, inasmuch as the [Armouchiquois] of that place are their great enemies [of the Souriquois and Etchemins]." With their supplies almost depleted, however, the expedition was forced to turn back before reaching the Kennebec River. Champlain later wrote that "this region is as disagreeable in winter as is that of our settlement [on St. Croix Island], in regard to which we were greatly deceived." The winter of 1604-05 was indeed to be anything but ordinary for the seventy-nine Frenchmen.

Island Prison

"I will always be of the opinion that whosoever goes into a country to possess it must not stay in the isles, there to be a prisoner," wrote Marc Lescarbot in his *Histoire de la Nouvelle France*.

Snow began falling on October 6, of which over a metre would remain until late April. The great tides of the Bay of Fundy, which rise and fall about fifteen metres in the area, made it too dangerous to cross to the mainland "on account of the great cakes of ice carried by the ebb and flow of the tide," which began floating by in early December. The cold was extreme in both its severity and length. As the men's health deteriorated, they could no longer row and haul the boats across the river—they became prisoners and the drawbacks of settling on the island were now keenly felt. The buildings were almost totally exposed to the fierce winter wind, and the men had almost no firewood. The liquors froze, except the Spanish wine, which was only portioned out on certain days of the week, while the cider had to be dispensed by the pound. They soon ran out of fresh drinking water and were "obliged to make use of very bad water and to drink melted snow...." Their diet consisted of salted meat and

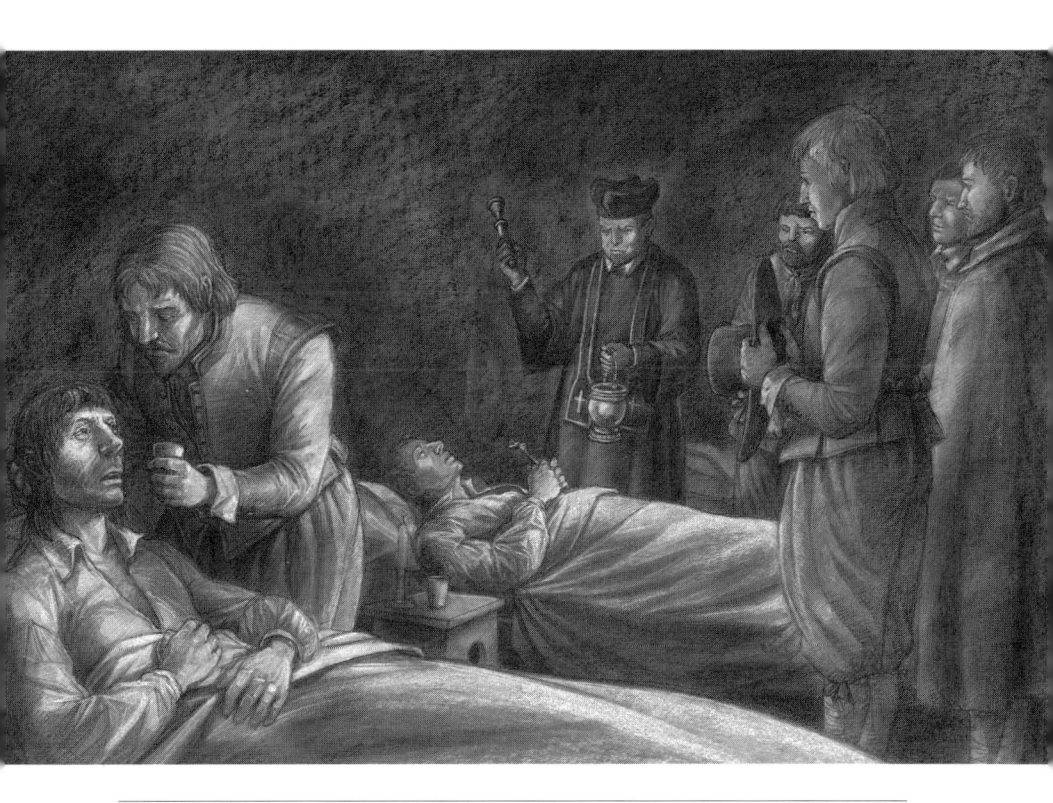

Thirty-five of the seventy-nine Frenchmen who wintered on St. Croix Island died of scurvy. Fewer would die of the disease at Port-Royal.

vegetables, since it was too painful to operate the hand-mill for grinding grain for making bread.

In the depth of winter's grip, many men became violently ill from "a certain malady…called land-sickness or scurvy," the most feared disease of all by those who winter in a cold climate. The stench of death began to fill the homes as the awful effects took hold:

There was engendered in the mouths of those who had it, large pieces of [excess] fungus flesh (which caused a great putrefaction); and this increased to such a degree that they could scarcely take anything except in very liquid form. Their teeth barely held in their places, and could be drawn out with the fingers without causing pain. This [excess] flesh was often cut away, which caused them to lose much blood from the mouth. Afterwards, they were taken with great pains in the arms and legs, which became swollen and very hard and covered with spots like flea-bites [from which flowed black clotted blood]; and they could not walk on account of the contraction of the nerves; consequently, they had almost no strength and suffered intolerable pains. They had also pains in the loins, stomach, and bowels, together with a very bad cough and shortness of breath. In brief, they were in such a state that the majority of the sick could neither get up nor move, nor could they even be held upright without fainting away.

By spring, thirty-five of the seventy-nine men had died, and more than twenty others were near death. Even those who had stayed well complained of minor pains and a shortness of breath. "For remedies there was none to be found...As for the tree called *annedda*, mentioned by the said [Jacques] Cartier, the [Amerindians] of these lands know not it." The *annedda* tree is thought to have been the white-cedar, which used to be known as the *arbor vitae*, or tree of life.

Amerindians (whom Passamaquoddy oral history says were their ancestors) passing by the island in March gave the French survivors some fresh game. With the availability of fresh food and drinking water and the warmer weather, the sick slowly regained their strength. Champlain later understatedly wrote: "It is difficult to know this country without having wintered there; for on arriving in summer everything is very pleasant on account of the woods, the beautiful landscapes, and the fine fishing... There are six months of winter in that country."

Searching for a Fitting Location

After the desperate winter, the survivors waited anxiously for the supply ships that had been expected by late April. That period came and went and "everybody began to have forebodings, fearing lest some accident had befallen them." Then, on June 15, Champlain, while on guard duty at about eleven o'clock at night, spotted a shallop approaching the island, from which came the familiar voice of François Gravé Du Pont. He had sailed ahead to tell them that the *Bonne Renommée* was only a short distance away, and that the Sieur des Antons of Saint-Malo in the *St.-Étienne* was following him with provisions and supplies. The next day the *Bonne Renommée* dropped anchor off the island, to the roar of the welcoming cannon fire and immense joy of those who had survived the winter.

Having perhaps now experienced what the Marquis de La Roche's men had discovered earlier on Sable Island, de Mons wasted little time implementing his plan for moving the settlement farther south. On June 18, he set out with Champlain, several other gentlemen, twenty sailors, and a Mi'kmaw guide named Panoniac and his Armouchiquois wife, who would be very helpful since they were going to her people's territory (ethnologist Ruth Holmes Whitehead speculates that she may have been a captured bride).

The expedition sailed along the coast to the Kennebec River area where they met Etchemin chief Météourmite. During their parley, which took place on the water, the chief told de Mons that he was willing to form an alliance with him and would be pleased if the French brought about reconciliation between him and his enemies. He also promised to tell two other chiefs, Marchin and Sasinou, who were away, about de Mons' mission. In gratitude, Sieur de Mons gave Météourmite a gift of biscuits and peas.

The French gradually made their way to the site of future Boston, then to port St Louis (Plymouth Harbour), next to Cap blanc (Cape Cod), and finally to nearby Malle-Barre (Nauset Harbour), where they had the first of several hostile encounters with the Armouchiquois of the area. Several men had gone ashore with large kettles (pots) to fetch fresh water. An Armouchiquois grabbed one of the kettles and ran off with it. Fearing that they were in danger, the French rushed back towards their pinnace[3] while several Armouchiquois who were in the boat leapt into the water, except for one whom the French had captured. Seeing this, their friends on shore "shot several arrows at [the Frenchman from whom the kettle had been snatched] from behind and brought him down. Perceiving his condition, they at once rushed upon him and dispatched him with their knives." The dead man was later buried and the Armouchiquois prisoner set free. With their supplies running low and after five weeks of sailing through increasingly bad weather, de Mons decided to return to St. Croix Island.

During their return trip, they visited with Armouchiquois Chief Marchin at the Chouacoit-R (Saco River, Maine). De Mons presented the chief, who

---

[3] A pinnace was favoured for exploration along the coast. It usually had two masts and was only partially decked over. It was normally transported in pieces on the larger vessel and then assembled upon arrival. A shallop, or long-boat, was basically a small row boat, which was housed on the deck of the ship. It was also sometimes towed behind the ship or pinnace (based on information by Elizabeth Jones).

had a reputation as "one of the mighty men of his country…" with gifts, and in return Chief Marchin handed over a young Etchemin boy who was being held prisoner.

The expedition arrived back at St. Croix Island on August 3 to find the *St.-Étienne* anchored in the river. There were now fresh supplies and about forty replacement workers, including masons, fishermen, sailors, caulkers, and tillers, as well as pilots Pierre Cramolet and Israel Bailleul, who had renewed their contracts for another year, and surgeon Guillaume Deschamps. But where were they going to settle next? On this matter de Mons made a swift decision. They would relocate to the expansive basin that they had seen the year before, the one that Champlain and Poutrincourt had liked so much—Port-Royal.

CHAPTER 3 *Port-Royal: A Promising Foothold*

"IN ORDER TO ESCAPE the cold and dreadful winter we experienced on Saint Croix Island...we outfitted two pinnaces to transport the woodwork of the homes on Saint Croix Island to [Port-Royal]... where we judged the climate to be much more agreeable and temperate."

In early August, Champlain and Gravé Du Pont went to Port-Royal to scout for a suitable location for the colony. They first considered a site at today's Annapolis Royal, but rejected it for being too far upriver and difficult to defend. They finally chose a rise of land on the north side of the riuiere de l'Equille (which by 1609 was being called the Rivière du Dauphin; now the Annapolis River), opposite today's Goat Island. Meanwhile, the workers dismantled most of the buildings on St. Croix Island, which, along with the equipment, stores, and men, were taken across the Bay of Fundy to Port-Royal.

Second Beginning

This time the French planted themselves firmly on the mainland where there were plenty of trees for construction and firewood, easy access to a variety of wild game, readily available fresh water, and fertile soil for planting gardens. Unlike at St. Croix Island, a large mountain range nearby would also provide protection against the cold north-west wind.

Like many early European outposts in northeastern North America, the Port-Royal Habitation was a plain quarters in a small wilderness clearing—part trading post and part fort. Champlain again drew up the plan for the settlement, which consisted of a compact group of buildings surrounding a central courtyard. A palisade and platform for four cannons, with clear views towards the harbour and up the river, were joined to the buildings for easy access.

In late August, with work on the settlement well underway, de Mons decided to return to France to arrange for supplies and to counteract the competing merchants' efforts to have his monopoly revoked. Along with twenty-two bales of furs, de Mons collected "curiosities" to take back to France in hopes of stirring interest in this "exotic" land and to gain support for his enterprise. His menagerie included a live six-month-old female moose, a humming-bird, horseshoe crabs, moose antlers, a few dried-out muskrats, dead birds and their feathers, a merganser, a blue-jay, and a red-winged blackbird. There were also illustrations of the greatest "curiosity" of all, at least for Europeans—the strangely clothed Amerindians, along with examples of their bows that were "taller than a man," a hefty club, and a birch-bark canoe.

As he sailed from Port-Royal in early September, de Mons likely did not imagine that he would never return to Acadie. Gravé Du Pont took charge of the approximately forty-five men, including three of the St. Croix Island survivors who, undaunted by their past experience, volunteered for a second winter: namely, Champlain, Champdoré, and Fougeray de Vitré. It seems the second Catholic priest and the Protestant minister also stayed on.

A person whom some authors place in de Mons' expedition of 1604-1605 was one Mathieu de Coste (or Da Costa), an interpreter of African descent sought after by both the French and Dutch to help them trade with the Amerindians. There is, however, no evidence of de Coste being at St. Croix Island nor at the Port-Royal Habitation. De Coste likely sailed on many voyages throughout the Atlantic region in the late 1500s and early 1600s, and probably spoke several languages, including "pidgin Basque," a dialect used in trading with the Amerindians. Some would later mistake him for a Black man who died of scurvy aboard the *Jonas* in 1606. However, it could not have been de Coste because two years later de Mons engaged him to work in "Canada, Acadie and elsewhere." Since by this time de Mons was operating in the St. Lawrence River area, if

Copperplate engraving likely based on a rough, yet approximately accurate, drawing by Champlain of the Port-Royal Habitation

MODERN LEGEND
(A) Artisans' dwellings; (B) Cannon platform; (C) Storehouse; (D) Dwelling of Sieur de Pont-Gravé (i.e. Gravé Du Pont) and Champlain; (E) Blacksmith shop; (F) Palisade; (G) Oven; (H) Kitchen; (I) Gardens; (K) Cemetery; (L) River; (M) Drainage ditch; (NN) Dwellings; (O) Small building used to store the rigging for the pinnaces became Sieur du Boulay's dwelling; (P) Habitation entrance. *
* Letter "P" is not on the original plan, but the entrance is evident by its design.

de Coste had crossed the Atlantic, he would probably have gone to Canada (Quebec).

Once again, the colonists tried to be agriculturally self-sufficient, as the vegetables and crops flourished in the fertile soil. Champlain, in a singularly unguarded moment of enthusiastic prose, described his garden as a kind of Shangri-La:

I surrounded [my garden] with ditches full of water wherein I placed some very fine trout; and through it flowed three brooks of very clear running water from which the greater part of our settlement was supplied...This spot was completely surrounded by meadows, and there I arranged a summerhouse with fine trees, in order that there I may enjoy the fresh air. I constructed there likewise a small reservoir to hold salt-water fish, which we took out, as we required them...

Around mid-September, ever hopeful of finding precious minerals, Champlain sailed with miner Maître Jacques to once again look for the elusive copper mine. They found Etchemin (Wolastoqiyik) chief Secoudon

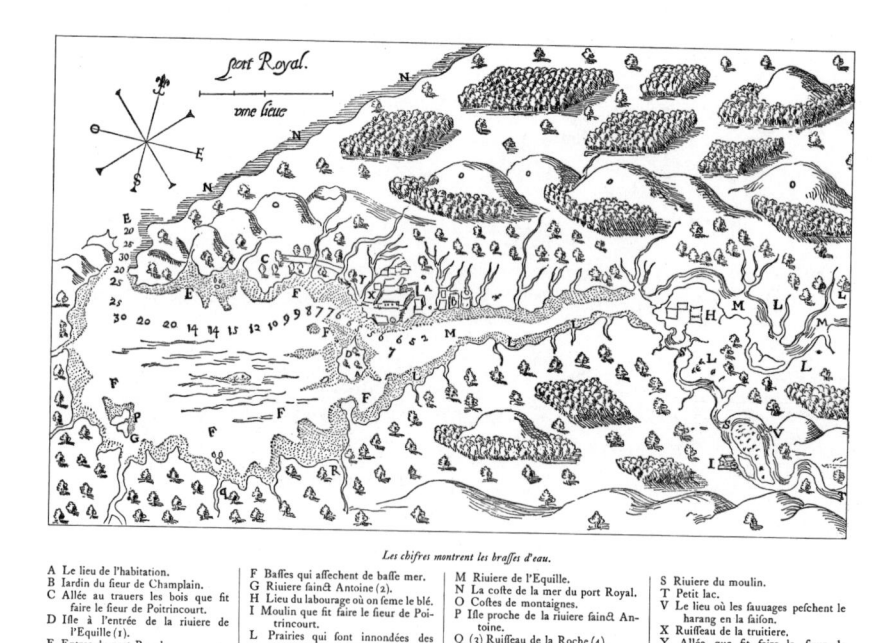

A map by Champlain showing: (A) Habitation opposite Goat Island; (B) Champlain's garden; (H) where wheat was grown at today's Annapolis Royal; (I) the gristmill on the Allain River; and (V) where Mi'kmaq fished for herring.

34 ✌ PORT-ROYAL HABITATION

at his village on the St. John River. (At this time, the Wolastoqiyik seem to have been principally located in today's southwestern New Brunswick.) Chief Secoudon guided them to an outcropping of copper in the Port des mines (Advocate Harbour, Nova Scotia) area. Champlain was again disappointed, however, since they "found there, embedded in grayish and red rocks, a few small bits of copper about as thick as a [penny], and others thicker." The copper was also not easily accessible because the Bay of Fundy tides covered it twice a day. Champlain and crew returned Chief Secoudon to his village and they sailed back to Port-Royal to prepare for the second winter in Acadie.

District of Kespukwitk

Mi'kmaw oral history says that the area the French called Port-Royal was in Kespukwitk (meaning "Lands End"), one of seven traditional Mi'kmaw hunting and fishing districts.

For at least three thousands years before the arrival of the French, the Mi'kmaq had lived a semi-nomadic existence, in extended family groups, moving between areas within Kespukwitk according to the cycle of the seasons and the availability of food sources. The rivers, including

Re-creation of a traditional Mi'kmaw summer encampment

Re-creation of a Mi'kmaw family travelling by canoe in the era before the arrival of Europeans

the Te'wapskik (Annapolis River), and lakes were their "highways" that allowed them to travel between the district's south and north coast, by way of what is now Kejimkujik National Park and National Historic Site. During these travels, the Mi'kmaq and their ancestors camped at today's Annapolis Royal.

Saqamaw, or Chief, Membertou lived with his followers in the St. Mary's Bay area, where they hunted and fished along its shores, and in the river and harbour of Port-Royal. Membertou, who was also a shaman, or medicine man, was described by Father Biard as "the greatest, most renowned and most formidable [Amerindian] within the memory of man...bearded like a Frenchman, although scarcely any of the others have hair upon their chin; grave and reserved; feeling a proper sense of dignity for his position as commander..." Lescarbot wrote that Membertou had "sufficient power to harangue, advise and lead [his people] to war, to render justice to one who has grievance, and like matters. He does not impose taxes upon his people but if there are profits from [hunting], he has a share of them, without being obliged to take part in it."

Membertou was purportedly around one hundred years old at this time; he claimed to have met Jacques Cartier in the mid-1530s. Like all good chiefs, Membertou put the well-being of his people first. He shared his food with the poor, even with those in other villages, and he "provided dogs for the chase, canoes for transportation, provisions and reserves for bad weather and expeditions." He would demonstrate a similar generosity towards the French.

The Mi'kmaq and the French were likely unaware of just how much they were going to affect each other. The genuine warmth and loyalty that developed between Membertou and the French formed the basis of a Mi'kmaq-French alliance that was to endure for over 150 years.

Turning a Corner

When snow began falling on December 20, 1605, the approximately forty-five inhabitants of Port-Royal were better prepared to deal with the winter than those who had wintered on St. Croix Island the year before, even though several men were already sick with the dreaded scurvy.

The buildings were better built, although the dampness still managed to enter the buildings from beneath the floorboards. They had an abundance of firewood and plenty of food had been preserved. The men were also able to grind wheat with the hand-mill so they had fresh bread. Nearby brooks provided fresh drinking water, but much to their dismay, they ran out of wine. The Mi'kmaq continued their customary visits, often bringing furs and fresh meat to trade for knives, axes, pots, beads, and even bread, which they greatly liked. Due to frequent rains, the

Illustration of the interior of the storerooms at St. Croix Island and Port-Royal [right] Type of hand-mill used by the French for grinding wheat

PORT-ROYAL: A PROMISING FOOTHOLD 37

Artistic interpretation of the priest leaving his dwelling

winter remained relatively mild. On February 20, however, there "blew so great a gale that a large number of trees were blown down, roots and all…it was a strange sight to behold."

Yet even with the improved living conditions, twelve men died of scurvy, including the miner, Maître Jacques, and the Catholic priest and Protestant minister, who had been constantly arguing since leaving France in March of 1604: "I [Champlain] have seen our curé and the minister fall to with fists on questions of faith…This was their way of settling points of controversy. I leave it to you to judge if it was a pleasant thing to see…the [Mi'kmaq and other Amerindians] were sometimes on one side, sometimes on the other, and the French mixed in according to their respective beliefs…."

Ironically, this was actually a relatively peaceful time between Protestants and Catholics in France, following the Peace of Religion in 1598, which included the famous Edict of Nantes granting Protestants freedom of conscience, equality of rights, and freedom to worship at specific locations. An unproven story told years later claimed that the men at Port-Royal had "laid [the priest and minister] in the same grave, to see if in death they would remain at peace, since living they had been unable to agree."

Surgeon Guillaume Deschamps performed autopsies on several of the men who had died of scurvy to determine what had caused the illness. But, like his predecessor at St. Croix Island, he could provide neither a diagnosis nor a remedy. Even so, the French at Port-Royal were slowly adapting to their surroundings.

Ever ready for adventure, Champlain, Gravé Du Pont, and a small crew left their settlement in mid-March "to proceed on a voyage of discovery along the coast of Florida," by which they meant what we would call the Atlantic seaboard of the United States. During the first night, strong winds snapped the boat's moorings, allowing it to drift perilously towards the rocks. But just when the situation appeared hopeless, a huge wave carried the boat over the shoal, dropping it on the sandy beach without anyone being injured. Champdoré, the boat's master, who was also a shipwright, quickly repaired the damage and they continued, although thick fog and strong headwinds soon forced them back to Port-Royal. On arrival, Gravé Du Pont suffered a heart attack, yet ten days later they set out again, since he felt that "the change of air would restore him to health." Gravé Du Pont appointed Champdoré master of the vessel; however, disaster struck once more.

The expedition had stopped for the night near the passage now called the Digby Gut, between the harbour of Port-Royal and the Bay of Fundy. By morning they were shrouded in thick fog and rain, and so Champdoré asked Gravé Du Pont whether they should proceed. From below deck, Du Pont told Champdoré to use his own judgement; the latter ordered the anchor raised and they headed towards the passage. But suddenly, the unpredictable tide carried them through the entrance and instantly they were on the rocks. While they managed to save themselves and most of the supplies, the pinnace was smashed to pieces. By sheer chance, Wolastoqiyik chief Secoudon, from the St. John River area, and some of his followers were nearby and, as Champlain later wrote, "We were very happy to have saved ourselves, and returned to our settlement with…[the Wolastoqiyik in their canoes], who remained [at Port-Royal] the greater part of the winter." Champlain harshly criticized Champdoré, saying, "This was a great disaster and [showed] a lack of foresight on the part of the master, who was obstinate and little versed in seamanship…"

When they reached the Habitation, Gravé Du Pont held what was doubtlessly the earliest semi-judicial inquiry in Acadie. He found Champdoré guilty of running the pinnace aground with "malicious intent"; he was then shackled and locked up. Yet if anyone were responsible for the mishap, it was surely Gravé Du Pont for having appointed Champdoré master. They had all been at Cape Cod the year before when Champdoré and pilot Pierre Cramolet misplaced a buoy marker and only narrowly avoided a shipwreck. His imprisonment, however, was to be short-lived.

Desperation and Jubilation

When the relief ship had not arrived by mid-June, Champdoré was freed temporarily so that he could "finish the pinnace which was on the stocks; and this duty he discharged well." Gravé Du Pont intended to go to Canso or Cape Breton to find a French ship to take them back to France. On July 17, two boats with about thirty passengers and crew departed Port-Royal as planned, leaving behind two so-called volunteers named La Taille and Miquelet. They had agreed to take care of the Habitation in return for fifty silver crowns and fifty more to the men's representatives on coming to get them the following year. Chief Membertou promised to take care of them and "that they should be no more unhappy than if they were his own children...." Back in France, meanwhile, de Mons was finally able to contract for a ship and supplies and to hire numerous workers.

The Sieur de Mons had decided to remain in France to continue the fight against the rival merchants who were still trying to have his monopoly revoked. So he asked Jean de Poutrincourt, who had gone with him to Acadie in 1604, to replace Gravé Du Pont as his lieutenant at Port-Royal. Poutrincourt agreed, despite, or perhaps because of, his ongoing financial and legal problems.

Poutrincourt tried to find a Catholic priest to replace the one at Port-Royal, not knowing that he was already dead; it being Holy Week, however, none was willing to leave. Nonetheless, he did recruit another participant, his invaluable ally and friend Marc Lescarbot, a lawyer and noted poet and writer. He had recently lost a case due to a dishonest judge and so wanted "to fly from a corrupt world" and to see the other side of the ocean first-hand.

On May 13, 1606, the *Jonas*, under the command of Captain Foulques, who had also been to Acadie in 1604, sailed towards the open seas and "little and little we lost sight of the great towers and town of La Rochelle...bidding France farewell."

It was an uneventful journey, except for Poutrincourt who spent the entire trip in his bunk suffering from seasickness. They stopped on the grand Banc des Morües (Grand Banks) to fish for cod, from whose guts, hearts, and other parts they "did mince with lard and spices; and with those things did make as good Bologna sausages as any can be made in Paris, and we did eat of them with a very good stomach." The men also caught dogfish, the skins of which the joiners would later use to smooth their woodwork. At least one man died during the crossing, for, Lescarbot wrote, "Monsieur de Poutrincourt made a negro to be [dissected] that died of [scurvy] in our voyage, who was found to have the inward parts very sound except the stomach, that had wrinkles, as though they were ulcered."

Around mid-July, Poutrincourt and company reached Canso, where they met a group of Mi'kmaq, who it seems had spent time at Port-Royal, since they told the French about "all that had passed [the] year before at Port Royal (whither we were bound)." This was confirmed by some men from Saint-Malo who were also at Canso. Since the French were headed to Port-Royal, one of the Mi'kmaq offered to go "through the woods, with a promise to be there within six days, to [advise Gravé Du Pont] of our coming...." There is no indication whether his offer was accepted. On July 23, the *Jonas* arrived at Port Mouton, where the men went ashore to gather firewood and fresh water. They also found "the cabins and lodgings, yet whole and unbroken, that of Monsieur de [Mons] made two years before."

Gravé Du Pont, meanwhile, had met with trouble as he and the others from Port-Royal were sailing towards Canso. During their first night, only the crew's skill saved them from crashing into the rocky shoals when the anchor cable of one of the boats broke. Then a heavy swell broke the rudder of the other boat, leaving the passengers in a life-threatening predicament. Gravé Du Pont released the still-shackled Champdoré, who skilfully repaired the rudder. After pleadings from the crew, Gravé Du Pont reluctantly set Champdoré free, having now atoned for his mistakes. On July 24, the expedition came upon de Mons' secretary, Ralleau, who had sailed along the coast to let them know that the *Jonas* was on its way.

Three days later the *Jonas* dropped anchor in front of the Habitation. The two Frenchmen inside, however, did not notice the ship until Chief Membertou "came to the French fort...crying as a madman, saying in his

An artistic interpretation of the Port-Royal Habitation, Acadie.

language: 'What! You stand here a-dining...and do not see a great ship that cometh here, and we know not what men they are.'" Membertou, along with one of his daughters, paddled out in a canoe to greet the new arrivals, while La Taille and Miquelet rushed to the cannon platform. But on seeing the white banner flying atop the mast as being French, they saluted a welcome with cannon fire and the *Jonas* replied in kind. The new arrivals "viewed the [Habitation], and...passed that day in giving God thanks, in seeing the [Mi'Kmaw] cabins, and walking through the meadow." Ralleau, Gravé Du Pont and their crews arrived at Port-Royal on July 30, and in celebration Poutrincourt opened a hoghead of wine in the courtyard where all indulged liberally "until their caps turned round."

While de Mons had been struggling to send out men and provisions throughout what is now Atlantic Canada, traders had continued to undermine his enterprise. When the *Jonas* was at Canso, for example, "men of Saint-Malo...who did deal for the associates of Monsieur [de Mons] complained that Basques, or men from [Saint-Jean-de-Luz]...had trucked with the [Amerindians, doubtlessly Mi'kmaq of Cape Breton] and carried away above six thousand beavers' skins." Rival merchants and traders would continue to undermine de Mons' efforts.

Baker putting bread into the bake oven

Blacksmith and armourer working in the forge

The Morning Toilet

Men rising and getting ready
for the day

Re-enactment of a Mi'kmaw girl gathering shellfish

Fishing weirs are still used today in the tidal coastal waters of the Bay of Fundy.

Routine of Daily Life

Among the recently arrived skilled artisans, or workers, at Port-Royal were carpenters Jean Pussot and Daniel Hay, joiners Antoine Esnault and Jean Hanin, pit-sawyers Oliver Bresson and Husson Jabart, locksmiths Jean Duval and Louis Fey, stonecutters (the largest group) Pierre Rondeau and Pierre Vozelles, toolmaker François Guitard, and tailors Toussaint Husson and Claude Desbry. Typically, the workers signed one-year contracts, at which time they received an advance on their wages, with the remainder to be paid at the end of their terms. Several contracts also stipulated that the workers were to receive a beaver felt hat or coat when they returned to France. In return, the men agreed to practice their trades and perform other tasks, while de Mons was to provide them with food and lodgings. Wages for the term of work generally varied from a low of 60 livres for the tailors, to 100 livres for the apothecary and most masons, to a high of 160 livres for the toolmaker François Guitard.

The workmen were required to work only three hours a day at their trades. Several even tried their hand at other crafts: some masons and stone-cutters successfully baked bread, while a pit-sawyer made charcoal for fuel. After they had completed their day's work, the men were free to do as they pleased, such as going hunting, fishing by boat or with nets, or gathering mussels, lobsters, or crabs along the shore. Lescarbot later fondly remembered one of de Mons' men who supplied the gentlemen's table: "we wanted [for] no fowl, bringing…sometimes…many mallards, or wild geese…[and] other kinds of birds."

Some of the other new arrivals at the Habitation included Poutrincourt's son, Charles de Biencourt, the former's cousin Claude de Saint-Étienne de La Tour and his son Charles, surgeon Estienne, apothecary Louis Hébert (related to Poutrincourt through marriage), Sieur du Boulay, who had been on the 1604 voyage with de Mons, Robert Gravé Du Pont (hereafter Pont-Gravé), son of François, Sieur Sourin "superintendent of building" and François Ardamin "provider to Poutrincourt's table."

Life at Port-Royal became orderly under Poutrincourt's direction. He quickly put men to work cleaning the houses or working at their trades, while others were sent upriver, in the area of today's Annapolis Royal, to plant wheat, rye, and other crops. Not only did these and the crops near the Habitation thrive, but within days of a second planting, sprouts appeared of grains, turnips, radishes, cabbages, and other crops. Lescarbot especially enjoyed working the soil: "I never made so much bodily work for the pleasure that I did take in [tilling] my garden…To sow wheat, barley, rye, oats, beans, peas, garden-herbs, and to water them—so much desire had I to know the goodness of the ground by my own experience." The fertile soil was enriched further with manure from the hogs' dung, seashells, and the leftovers from the kitchen. Biencourt also had his own garden in which he grew "oranges and citrons, they sprung plants of a foot high at three months' end…."

The French also planted hemp, from which they made rope that was attached to the iron hooks used as a trade item with the Mi'kmaq and other Amerindians. They also made soap from wood ash, which they used to whiten linen.

An astrolabe purportedly used by Samuel de Champlain

Near the Habitation, and during their voyages, the men gathered wild blueberries, strawberries, raspberries, gooseberries, apples for making marmalade, and small seaweed peas. The rivers and bays teemed with mussels, scallops, cockles, sea-chestnuts, crabs, and lobsters. The French were particularly impressed with the Mi'kmaw fishing weirs:

For the dolphins, sturgeons, and salmons do get to the head of the river in the said Port Royal where such quantity of them are that they carried away the nets which we laid for them...The [Mi'kmaq] do make a hurdle or weir, that [crosses] the brooks, which they hold almost straight propped against wooden bars, archwise and leave [an opening] for the fishes to pass, which [when the tide recedes] all the fish is found stayed in such multitude that they suffer to be lost...they took [the fish] in this manner or by harping irons.

These local provisions were augmented with foods brought from France, such as rice, prunes, olive oil, vinegar, almonds, lemon peel, raisins, spices, sugar-loafs, peas, beans, hams, dry cod, and salt beef.

Before leaving France, de Mons had instructed Poutrincourt to

Detail from Champlain's illustration of the "battle" with the Armouchiquois at port fortuné (Stage Harbour, Chatham, Cape Cod)

A Le lieu où estoient les François faisans le pain.
B Les sauuages surprenans les François en tirant sur eux à coups de flèches.
C François bruslez par les sauuages.
D François s'enfuians à la barque tout lardés de flèches.
E Troupes de sauuages faisans brusler les François qu'ils auoient tués.
F Montaigne sur le port.
G Cabannes des sauuages.
H François à terre chargeans les sauuages.
I Sauuages desfaicts par les François.
L Chaloupe où estoient les François.
M Sauuages autour de la chaloupe qui furent surpris par nos gens.
N Barque du sieur de Poitrincourt.
O Le port.
P Petit ruisseau.
Q François tombez morts dans l'eau pensans se sauuer à la barque.
R Ruisseau venant de certins marescages.
S Bois par où les sauuages venoient à couuert.

p. 258

48 ❧ Port-Royal Habitation

relocate the settlement to a more suitable climate farther south; as with St. Croix Island, de Mons considered Port-Royal a temporary location. Originally, the idea was to remove the entire colony the next year, exploring as they went; however, Champlain says that: "with the approval of every one [they] decided to remain at Port Royal for this year, inasmuch as nothing had been discovered since the Sieur de [Mons'] voyage, and the four months which remained before winter were not sufficient to seek a new site and make another settlement…we should merely discover some more [suitable] situation for the [settlement]."

To this end, Poutrincourt, Champlain, Pont-Gravé, Hébert, and several others left on an exploratory voyage in late August, while at the same time (François) Gravé Du Pont and the others who had wintered at Port-Royal departed for France in the *Jonas*. (Champlain, Champdoré, and Fougeray de Vitré had decided to once again remain in Acadie.) However, bad weather forced Poutrincourt's pinnace back to Port-Royal, while the larger ship continued its voyage. Four days later, with Lescarbot left in charge of the Habitation, they set out on a voyage that was to be full of hardship and mishaps.

Muskets, Arrows, and Deaths

At the mouth of the St. Croix River, Poutrincourt met Wolastoqiyik chief Secoudon and Mi'kmaw chief Messamouet, who were heading to the Saco River, Maine, where "they wished to go make an alliance with [the Armouchiquois] of the country by offering sundry presents." After visiting St. Croix Island, the French reached the Saco River on September 21, just as the Armouchiquois had finished harvesting their corn.

During Poutrincourt's parley with Chiefs Onemechin (whom Champlain had met the year before) and Marchin, the former handed over a Mi'kmaw, who was being held prisoner. Then Chief Messamouet began "with much vehemency and affection, with a gesture of the body and arms…" an almost hour-long speech in which he appealed to the Armouchiquois to form an alliance and to take advantage of the trade with the French, for he had been to France (before 1580) and knew the value of their goods. To demonstrate his friendship, Messamouet then threw all the items he had obtained in trading with the French, such as kettles, hatchets, knives, cloaks, and waistcoats, into Chief Onemechin's canoe. The next day, Onemechin reciprocated with presents of Indian corn, squashes, tobacco, and Brazilian beans but gave no speech. Messamouet was unimpressed,

Pen-and-ink rendering of the *Théâtre de Neptune*, performed on November 14, 1606

and he left in a huff, threatening to make war upon them before long. Meanwhile, Chief Secoudon continued south with the expedition.

Both Poutrincourt and Champlain were impressed with the harbour of what is today's Gloucester, Massachusetts: "This port is very beautiful and a good one, with water enough for vessels, and shelter behind the islands…we named it Le Beau port [Beautiful Port]." This was the only place along the coast that the French seriously considered as a possible site for permanent settlement. Yet, after almost a month, the expedition was no farther south than what had been explored the previous year. Their progress slowed further when the rudder broke, forcing them to stop at port fortuné (Stage Harbour, Chatham area, Cape Cod). During their two-week stay, Poutrincourt made contact with the local Armouchiquois, but rather than being welcomed they were met by armed fighters.

Poutrincourt, sensing they were in danger, ordered his men to return immediately to the pinnace, but three disobeyed. When he sent a shallop to retrieve them, the men again refused to leave, and were in fact joined on shore by two others. The next morning, hundreds of Armouchiquois attacked the men sleeping on shore, killing three instantly and severely wounding the two others, including the ringleader, locksmith Jean Duval. The French buried the dead near the cross they had set up the day before, the act of which likely raised the Armouchiquois' suspicions about their intentions. In a final display of contempt, Armouchiquois fighters then tore down the cross and dug up the bodies. The French re-interred the dead and re-erected the cross.

The expedition departed port fortuné (Stage Harbour)—which the French so named "on account of the misfortune which happened to us there"—but foul weather forced them to return. Their bad luck continued when Pont-Gravé severely injured a hand when his matchlock musket exploded. Then they had yet another confrontation with the Armouchiquois.

To avenge the killing of his men, Poutrincourt set a trap to capture several Armouchiquois fighters to take back to Port-Royal as slave labour. They lured the Armouchiquois to the water's edge, but sensing that it was a trap, the Armouchiquois quickly retreated although not before "six or seven of them were cut to pieces" by the French muskets. With supplies running low and the injured needing medical treatment, Poutrincourt decided to head back to Port-Royal.

These disastrous encounters with the Armouchiquois marked a pivotal turning point for the French: they effectively ended any plans the French may have had for "occupying" lands to the south. Instead, the region was soon to be claimed by England.

Bountiful Winter of Cheer

On November 14 a discouraged Poutrincourt and crew arrived back at Port-Royal, where, to their amazement, Neptune, god of the sea, greeted them in a either a canoe or a boat, surrounded by his Tritons and Amerindians, likely Mi'kmaq, in canoes. Some secondary sources speculate they were likely Frenchmen dressed up as Amerindians. Each in turn narrated the praises of the leaders and then sang in chorus the glory of the king, as trumpets blared and cannons echoed. These were characters from a play entitled the *Théâtre de Neptune*, which Lescarbot had hastily produced for the occasion, and as a way of occupying the men who feared the expedition had met with disaster. Just six weeks later, Shakespeare's *King Lear* would receive its first performance in England. Lescarbot's original play remains the first recorded theatrical production in present-day Canada.

When the rejoicing was over, Poutrincourt went upriver to inspect the crops while others prepared the gardens for the following spring. Apothecary Hébert treated the injured, including Pont-Gravé, whose damaged hand he wrapped in a plaster made from the same clay used to make bricks for the fireplaces and held together with fir tree gum melted in a furnace; this substance was also used to seal the joints in the boats that the French built at Port-Royal.

The warm homecoming, however, was suddenly disrupted when Etchemin (Passamaquoddy) chief Ouagimou arrived with the embalmed body of Panoniac, who had been off trading when he was killed in revenge for the deaths of several Armouchiquois men and a woman seemingly from the Saco River area, whom Etchemin fighters had apparently killed earlier near Mount Desert Island. Panoniac and his Armouchiquois wife had guided de Mons on a voyage the year before. A long, intricate mourning ritual followed: "As soon as the body was brought ashore, the relatives [encircled him]…their faces being painted all over with black. After a great deal of weeping, they took a quantity of tobacco and two or three dogs and other things belonging to the deceased, and burnt them [near] our settlement."

A re-creation of a traditional Mi'kmaw winter encampment in the time before European contact.

Chief Membertou wrapped the body in a beautiful red coverlet that Champlain had given him. He then gave a rousing speech inciting his friends and followers to go to war against the Armouchiquois, which they vowed to do come spring. According to Lescarbot (and Champlain), Membertou had a reputation of being a fierce fighter: "He hath been very great warrior in his young age, and bloody during his life; which is the cause why he is said to have many enemies...." Some of the French speculated that this was also why Membertou stayed close to their settlement because he appreciated the security their firearms provided, while the French were equally grateful to have the support of such an influential chief. Following Membertou's speech, Panoniac was moved to his parents' wigwam. They wrapped him tightly in a moose hide to preserve the body for the winter. (In the spring—before Membertou launched his war of revenge—Panoniac, according to Mi'kmaw custom, was buried at a secret location on a desolate island in the Cape Sable area, where his enemies could not find him.)

An assortment of trade goods that the Mi'kmaq and other Amerindians received in exchange for their furs.

One of numerous artistic representations of Samuel de Champlain

Artistic interpretation of Marc Lescarbot writing in his room at the Habitation, 1606-07

54 ❧ Port-Royal Habitation

By now, life at the Habitation had taken on an air of peasant domesticity, despite the total absence of European women: hogs were allowed to roam freely, the hens and pigeons multiplied and produced plenty of eggs (much to the men's frustration, marauding eagles would swoop down and snatch the pigeons for food), and the lone sheep produced fine wool. The French, however, had brought one unwelcome creature with them on their ships: the rat, of which Lescarbot says that they "had an ample provision…and made unceasing warfare on them. The [Mi'kmaq and other Amerindians] had no knowledge of these animals before our coming; but in our time they have been beset by them, since from our fort they went even to their lodges…to eat or suck their fish oils."

To keep active as winter approached, Champlain, assisted by several labourers, began cutting a path through the forest to create a shaded promenade. On seeing this, Poutrincourt ordered that another one be cut through the woods as a more direct route to the entrance to the port, but it was never completed.

Snow arrived in late December, yet it remained fairly mild. Lescarbot said that in January of 1607, they could walk around without their heavy cloaks and that they picnicked upriver and "did dine merrily in the sunshine." There was also plenty of bread and everyone received one and a half pints "of pure and good wine a day." It was felt that wine was also "a sovereign preservative against the sickness of this country (namely scurvy)." The warmer winter, however, was disastrous for the Mi'kmaq, whom Champlain says "suffered a severe famine" because they could not capture as many moose, a main food staple, as customary by running them down in the snow. Poutrincourt fed some Mi'kmaq, including Membertou and his immediate family. Nonetheless, the Mi'kmaq were still able to bring pelts—beaver, muskrat, otter, moose, fox, seal—to the Habitation to trade for goods. European technology and trade items continued to interest and intrigue the Mi'kmaq because they were so useful.

The Mi'kmaq valued especially the European-made metal axes and kettles (pots), particularly the copper ones, which they found practical and useful compared to their large, fixed-location wooden cooking "kettles." Europeans, however, had more difficulty understanding Mi'kmaw preferences for other objects, such as mirrors, metals, and glass beads of a certain type and colour; as historian Olive Dickason notes: "These objects substituted for traditional shiny metals, crystals, quartzite, and certain types of shells, all believed to possess a quality relating to the fundamental nature of the universe in its physical and spiritual aspects."

While the French and other Europeans may not have understood this "other-worldly" characteristic, they quickly recognized which goods inspired the Mi'kmaq and other Amerindians to trade with them.

The French at Port-Royal (and elsewhere) were equally fascinated with Mi'kmaw technology, such as their well-made birch-bark canoes, snowshoes, toboggans, and moccasins, which they adopted because nothing Europeans could supply was as ideally suited to a northern environment.

The introduction of European technology would gradually, but pervasively, change the lives of the Mi'kmaq and other Amerindians. The change may have been greater among the Mi'kmaq than for other inland Amerindian societies because their contacts were generally earlier and more intensive as year-round contact by ship was possible. Historian Cornelius Jaenen writes, for example, that, "The pressures on the [Mi'kmaw] women to prepare hides and skins for the French trade meant that there was less time available for preparing food, clothing, and household items for their subsistence." Over time, the Mi'kmaq and other Amerindians would come to depend a great deal on both European goods and food, to the great detriment of their traditional life skills.

During the winter of 1607, Lescarbot kept himself intellectually occupied: "Concerning the labour of the mind, I took reasonable part of it, at the night, everyone being retired, among the [babbling], noises, hurlyburlies, I was shut up in my study, reading or writing of something." In fact, Lescarbot began one of the earliest detailed treatises on the life and customs of the Mi'kmaq, which would be published as part of his book, *Histoire de la Nouvelle France*, in 1609. Lescarbot thought very highly of the Mi'kmaq (and other Amerindians), describing them as having "courage, fidelity, generosity, and humanity...So if we commonly call them Savages, the word is abusive and unmerited, for they are anything but that..." He wrote on diverse topics, such as the Mi'kmaw custom with tobacco: "For we have many times seen [Amerindian] strangers to arrive in Port Royal, who being landed, without [a word] went to Membertou's cabin, where they sat down taking tobacco, and having well drunken of it, did give the tobacco-pipe to him that seemed to be the worthiest person, and after consequently to the others. Then some half an hour after they did begin to speak." He also described an incident invovling several Armouchiquois as prisoners. One day it was discovered that one, a woman, had helped a fellow-prisoner to escape; and to help him on his way had stolen a tinderbox and hatchet from Membertou's wigwam. As punishment, a group of Mi'kmaw women took her some distance from Port-Royal where they killed her. That, Lescarbot observed, "is their form of justice." Since there was no priest or minister, Lescarbot, at Poutrincourt's request, also gave the men "Christian instructions" on Sundays, which apparently had little impact.

Champlain also worked at preparing his maps and notes about his explorations and what he had observed and learned from the Amerindians.

Cook and servant boy tending the meat on the fireplace spit

[far page] Artistic interpretation of the Order of Good Cheer

After two winters in Acadie, experience had taught Champlain that those who had been active seemed to have suffered the least from scurvy. So he established *l'ordre de [bon temps]*, or the Order of Good Cheer, which he said was "more profitable than all sorts of medicine we might have used." It was an elaborately staged event, performed by the approximately fifteen gentlemen who sat at Poutrincourt's table.

For there was none but (two days before his turn came) was careful to go a-hunting or fishing…for it was the great banquet, where the Governor of the feast or Steward (whom the [Amerindians] do call atoctegic*) having made the cook to make all things ready, did march with his napkin on his shoulder and his staff of office in hand, with the collar of the office around his neck…and all of them of the order following of him, bearing every one a dish…And at night after grace was said, he resigned the collar of the order, with a cup of wine, to his successor in that charge, and they drank one to the other…we had an abundance of fowl…caribous (or deer), beavers, otters, bears, rabbits, wild-cats and such like, which the [Amerindians] did take, wherewith we made as good dishes of meat as the cook's-shops that be in the Rue aux Ours and greater store; for of all meats none is…so delicate as the beaver's tail. Yea, we have had sometimes half a dozen sturgeons at one clap, which the [Amerindians] did bring to us.…In such actions we had always twenty or thirty [Amerindians], men, women, girls, boys, who [watched] us doing our offices. Bread was given gratis.…But as for [Chief] Membertou and other [Chiefs] (when they came to us) they sat at the table eating and drinking as we did; and we took pleasure in seeing them, as [conversely] their absence was irksome unto us.…*

The improved living conditions seem to have paid off, for by spring only four men had died of scurvy—the colonists were slowly adapting.

Betrayals and Sorrowful Departure

In April 1607, Poutrincourt had two boats readied so that they could go to Canso to seek passage on ships heading back to France, should the relief ship not arrive as scheduled. Meanwhile, he had a water-mill built on today's Allain River to lessen the burden of grinding wheat by hand. The mill was located in the same area where the French had been making charcoal for the blacksmith's forge, and it was also where the Mi'kmaq fished for the bountiful alewives (a species of herring). Damming the river produced another benefit: alewives swimming upriver were trapped in such quantities that Poutrincourt had two casks of them and one of sardines salted to take back to France as evidence of Acadie's prosperity.

On May 24, however, a Captain Chevalier arrived from Canso with devastating news. With help from the all-powerful Duc de Sully—one of Henri IV's ministers who had opposed the use of monopolies, believing that overseas colonization in a northern climate would never pay the huge outlays—rival merchants and fishing interests in France had finally persauded the king to revoke de Mons' fur-trading monopoly. The men at Port-Royal had, therefore, been ordered to pack up and go to Canso where the *Jonas* was fishing for cod. The only bit of good news they heard was of the birth of the Duc d'Orleans, Henri IV's second son, which they celebrated with a bonfire, a firing of cannons and muskets, and a song.

Following this brief respite, the men began the dreary task of preparing to leave Port-Royal. At the same time, Poutrincourt sent Captain

Champlain's illustration of the Armouchiquois from his 1612 map of New France.

Chevalier, Champdoré, and Lescarbot to the St. John and St. Croix River areas to trade for furs while he and Champlain went to search for the ever-elusive copper mines.

In the meantime, Chief Membertou launched his war against the Armouchiquois. In early June, following a customary parley, he led a sizeable force of fighters "away from the dwelling that [he] had newly made at [Port-Royal] in the form of a town, compassed about with high [wooden stakes]..." to the Saco River to avenge the killing of Panoniac the previous year. Wolastoqiyik chief Secoudon, who was assembling a war party in the St. John River area—which included Amerindians (Mi'kmaq among them) from as far away as Gaspé—would also join them.

After a meeting with Chief Secoudon, before he joined Membertou's war party, Captain Chevalier and crew sailed to St. Croix Island where they, according to Lescarbot, "found...the buildings left there all whole, saving that the storehouse was uncovered on one side...As for the gardens, we found coleworts, sorrel, lettuces, which we used for our kitchen." But Lescarbot was unimpressed with some of the French sailors who burned the casks that were in the courtyard; he felt that the Amerindians were more "humane and honest" than they since the former had not "taken so much as a piece of wood, nor salt, which was there in quantity...." While in the area, the French also met Etchemin (Passamaquoddy) chief Ouagimou, who was also preparing to join Membertou's war party.

At the end of July, with everything packed away, two groups of men, including Chevalier, Lescarbot, and Champdoré, departed for Canso. Poutrincourt, Champlain, and eight others delayed their departure in order to gather samples of rye and wheat to take back to France.

Just as the French were about to leave, however, Membertou arrived back from the Saco River, victorious over the Armouchiquois. During the battle, the French metal-tipped spears and arrows, and above all the swords, cutlasses (curved swords used by sailors), and even muskets used by some of Membertou's fighters had apparently been devastating against the Armouchiquois' traditional arrows. Champlain says that during the war, Armouchiquois chiefs Onemechin and Marchin were killed by Etchemin chief Sasinou, who was subsequently killed by followers of the two former chiefs. While some fighters in Membertou's war party were wounded, including Etchemin (Passamaquoddy) chief Ouagimou, none were apparently killed.

On August 11, Poutrincourt and the others finally departed Port-Royal. In a sign of friendship and respect, Poutrincourt left the Habitation in Membertou's care, giving him ten barrels of flour, free use of the buildings, and a promise that he would return the following year to stay.

The *Jonas*, with the Port-Royal settlers on board, put in at Roscoff in lower Brittany, France, in late October. It seems that the Amerindian travelling with them was wonder-struck at "the buildings, steeples, and windmills in France; yea, also of the women, whom he had never seen clothed after our manner." After four days, at Saint-Malo, Poutrincourt, Biencourt, and Lescarbot went to visit the fortress-like Abbey of Mont Saint-Michel, well known even then as a pilgrimage and tourist destination, where Lescarbot likely left some spruce gum for burning as incense, which he had brought from Port-Royal.

Their journey ended at Honfleur, where they bid each other farewell. Poutrincourt travelled to Paris where he presented the king with his gifts from Acadie—including five bustards (which ended up at the king's palace at Fontainebleau), and samples of corn, wheat, rye, barley and oats.

So it was that the French abandoned Port-Royal just three months after the English, under the auspices of the London Company, had founded Jamestown, Virginia, an event that would eventually see the French and English clash on the shores of Port-Royal.

In 1606, King James I of England had granted the Virginia Company of London and the Virginia Company of Plymouth each a part of the area between the 34th and 45th parallels. The companies' territory overlapped almost all of de Mons' grant.

After three years of effort and huge costs, de Mons grudgingly accepted that it was impossible for him to enforce his monopoly along Acadie's long and twisted coastline. Dutch, Spanish, and especially French vessels in considerable numbers were flouting the monopoly, while, unlike de Mons, not having to bear the enormous costs of settlement. Yet, the effort was not a complete failure. The French had acquired practical knowledge about the environment and geography of the Atlantic coast, and they had learned how to interact with the Mi'kmaq and other Amerindians. These lessons would be put to practical use by de Mons, Champlain, and Gravé Du Pont—and later even Louis Hébert—when they turned their interests towards Canada (Quebec) beginning in 1608. Ironically, the French abandoned Port-Royal just as real progress was being made at adapting to the environment. Indeed, Lescarbot felt, perhaps optimistically, that within a year they would have been be able to survive without help from France. Yet, the story of the Port-Royal Habitation did not end in 1607.

Artistic rendering of nobleman Jean de Biencourt de Poutrincourt et de Saint-Just

CHAPTER 4 *Seigneury of Port-Royal*

THOUGH THE FRENCH LEFT Port-Royal in a group in 1607, they did not completely abandon the Habitation for the next three years. While de Mons had lost his monopoly, he did not fully give up on Acadie either, despite his enormous financial losses. In the months that followed the French departure, Champlain persuaded de Mons that the most lucrative fur trade was along the St. Lawrence River and inland, and not in Acadie. To encourage his effort, Henri IV granted de Mons a one-year renewal of his original fur-trade monopoly, provided he established a post on the St. Lawrence River.

The Sieur De Mons "had two ships equipped at Honfleur and made [Champlain] his lieutenant...[François Gravé Du Pont] started first to go to Tadoussac, and [Champlain aboard the

Don-de-Dieu] went after him." Champlain explored to the narrowest part of the St. Lawrence River, where he founded Quebec in July of 1608. Simultaneously, de Mons had sent Jean Ralleau and Pierre Champdoré to Acadie to trade for furs. Membertou and his family happily welcomed them back to Port-Royal, but their stay at the Habitation was short-lived.

The French sailed to the Saco River, Maine, where they met Armouchiquois chief Asticou, who had replaced Chief Onemechin upon his death in Membertou's war. He diplomatically demanded that Champdoré send him a representative of the Etchemins to make peace with him. They were still hostile toward one another since Membertou's war a year earlier. As a result, Etchemin (Passamaquoddy) chief Ouagimou was chosen and peace was quickly concluded with due ceremony. While in the area, the French do not appear to have heard any news about the English settlement that had been established by the Plymouth Company at the mouth of the Kennebec River in 1607, but which had recently been abandoned.

Ralleau and Champdoré returned to France with a cargo of furs to report on what they had found and heard. But what had become of Poutrincourt, whom de Mons had appointed lieutentant-governor of Acadie?

Search for Backers and Deceit

In March of 1608, Henri IV ratified Sieur de Mons' signeurial grant of Port-Royal (which included fur-trading and fishing privileges) to Poutrincourt, provided that he moved there with several families to settle permanently. At the same time, the king approached Father Pierre Coton, his confessor, to obtain the services of the wealthy and powerful Society of Jesus (commonly known as Jesuits), "for the securing of the salvation of the [Amerindians]," to whom he promised financial support. The Jesuits' superiors chose Fathers Pierre Biard and Énemond Massé. Father Biard was soon dispatched to Bordeaux only to discover that no one knew of the venture and that there were "no preparations, no reports or tidings." But as we shall see, religious intrigue would delay the Jesuits' departure for almost three years.

As usual, Poutrincourt's finances were in shambles and neither the king nor private investors were willing to back the voyage. Even so, he persevered in his quest for the "glory of France" and hopefully himself. Meanwhile, Father Massé had become the confessor to the deeply religious noblewoman Antoinette de Pons, Marquise de Guercheville, wife of the governor of Paris and first lady-in-waiting to the queen. Massé no doubt acquainted her with the Jesuits' project, for she was to exert a determining behind-the-scenes influence on the events that were to unfold on both sides of the Atlantic.

Henri IV was unpleasantly surprised to learn in November of 1609 that Poutrincourt was still in Paris and had not yet gone to Acadie. The king called Poutrincourt to account, during which he assured his majesty that "he would take leave of him at once, to go directly and make preparations to leave immediately." Hearing of this, Father Coton went to meet with Poutrincourt. But being distrustful of the Jesuits—who were seen by many in France to be working for Spain, where the society originated—Poutrincourt told him that the kitchen at the Habitation had not been built (which was of course untrue) and that it would be better for the Jesuits to wait until the next year to set sail. Father Coton reluctantly accepted this "compromise." "Thereupon [Poutrincourt] left Paris and consumed the entire Winter in making preparations."

Poutrincourt Returns to His Manoir

After numerous false starts and disappointments, Poutrincourt was finally able to have a ship outfitted, engage a crew, and "gather together many worthy gentlemen and artisans," including his son Charles de Biencourt de Saint-Just (hereafter Biencourt), apothecary Louis Hébert, Thomas Robin, Vicomte de Coulogne—a heavy investor in the expedition—Claude Saint-Étienne de La Tour and his son, Charles Saint-Étienne de La Tour, along with about twenty workmen. Poutrincourt also acquired the services of Abbé Jessé Fléché, a secular priest, in hopes of impeding, if not stopping, the Jesuits from starting a mission in Acadie.

The *Grâce-de-Dieu* sailed from Dieppe in late February of 1610, loaded to the gunwales with furniture, goods, equipment, and munitions for Port-Royal. Three months later, after enduring both raging storms and days on end where there was virtually no wind, the expedition reached Acadie. Near Cape Sable, however, they were blown off course towards the Penobscot River, Maine. The expedition finally reached Port-Royal

Artist interpretation of apothecary Louis Hébert preparing medicines

around mid-June, almost three years since Poutrincourt had last been on its shores. They found the Habitation in good repair except for part of the roofs that had been damaged by storms. As well, the gardens were overgrown and the water-mill upriver needed repairs. The French were amazed to find that not a piece of furniture was missing, which was due mainly to Membertou's diligence; Olive Dickason notes: "An Amerindian custom that surprised early Europeans was that of respecting food caches and supply depots of others, even though unguarded."

Poutrincourt was anxious to send his son back to France with proof that progress was being made in "Christianizing" the Amerindians. So, with Biencourt acting as translator, he explained to Chief Membertou who Abbé Fléché was and why he was there. He put to the chief that he and his family should renounce the devil and accept the Christian God, which Membertou agreed to do. On June 24, 1610, Membertou and twenty members of his family were among the first Amerindians in North America to "adopt" Christianity. Abbé Fléché, surnamed "the Patriarch," baptized the chief Henri, after the now-deceased King Henri IV (they were unaware that he had been murdered in May), while he baptized Membertou's wife Marie, after the queen. The baptism of their children and other family members, who were each given a Christian name, soon followed. The details were carefully recorded in a registry that Biencourt was to take back to the king as proof of Poutrincourt's enthusiasm and to show that the Jesuits were not needed in Acadie. (By the time Father Fléché left Port-Royal in 1611, he had baptized approximately 140 Mi'kmaq and other Amerindians, most with little or no instruction in the faith.)

Biencourt, along with Thomas Robin, sailed from Port-Royal in early July with a few pelts, the precious baptismal registry, and a letter from Poutrincourt asking the king to grant him sole rights to the fur trade in Acadie, and that Biencourt be named vice-admiral with the powers to enforce the monopoly. Over twenty men remained at the Habitation.

During the summer and early fall, the men planted gardens, repaired the damaged buildings and water-mill and went fishing and hunting. To overcome the need to fetch drinking water from streams, they also dug a well in the Habitation's central courtyard, which provided excellent water. Abbé Fléché apparently occupied Lescarbot's former "study" and tended to the latter's still-flourishing vegetable and herb gardens.

Meanwhile in France, Biencourt and Thomas Robin had gone to Paris in late August where they presented the baptismal registry and

Poutrincourt's letter to the queen. Biencourt quickly realized, however, that the Jesuits had gained the upper hand within the Royal Court; Fathers Biard and Massé would be going with him to Port-Royal. While Biencourt was named the vice-admiral of Acadie, Poutrincourt did not receive a fur-trade monopoly.

When Fathers Biard and Massé arrived at Dieppe, the Huguenot merchants, Du Jardin and Du Quesne, who were outfitting the *Grâce-de-Dieu*, refused to allow the Jesuits to board unless "the queen would direct them to transport the whole order beyond the sea." The merchants, who associated the Jesuits with the Counter-Reformation that opposed Protestantism, told Biencourt that they would only take the Jesuits if he repaid the expenses they had incurred in preparing the vessel. Thomas Robin informed Mme de Guercheville of the "ultimatum." Incensed and unwilling "to see the efforts of hell prevail," she quickly raised the funds from "Nobles, Princes, and from all the Court." Under the partnership, Thomas Robin and Biencourt had allied themselves with the Jesuits, "for half of all and each of the merchandizes, victuals, instalments, and generally the whole cargo." Additionally, Mme de Guercheville granted Biard and Massé "a very fair viaticum [allowance]," while Henriette d'Entragues, Marquise de Vernueil provided the Jesuits with sacred vessels and robes, and Mme de Sourdis furnished them with linen for the altar.

The *Grâce-de-Dieu* sailed from Dieppe on January 26, 1611, with thirty-six on board—including Biencourt, Thomas Robin, and Fathers Biard and Massé—eighteen of whom had signed on to stay at Port-Royal.

By now, however, the supplies at Port-Royal were being rationed. There had been frequent and heated arguments, and "mutinies and conspiracies arose...the cook stole part of what belonged to others, while a certain one cried 'hunger' who [had] plenty of bread and meat in his [room]." On occasion, the Mi'kmaq provided fresh meat, but for almost seven weeks the French had survived almost solely on dried peas and beans. In fact, as the situation got worse Poutrincourt apparently sent some of his men to live with the Mi'kmaq. The remaining inhabitants at the Habitation were eventually reduced to eating ground nut roots or the pea-like plant provided by the Mi'kmaq.

In early March of 1611, a Mi'kmaw suddenly arrived at the Habitation with news that Membertou was dying. Poutrincourt found the chief inside his wigwam wrapped in his fine otter robe, waiting to die. A medicine man had advised the chief to stop eating because death was inevitable. As

Membertou's followers chanted and listened to people talk of his past life of valour and honour, his sons poured cold water on their father's bare stomach to hasten his death, because, Lescarbot speculated, "These being nomadic, and not being able to continue living in one place, cannot drag after them their fathers or friends, the aged or the sick." Poutrincourt had Membertou moved to the Habitation where "he had a good fire prepared for him, and, placing him near it upon a good bed, had him rubbed, nursed, well cared for, and doctored…at the end of three days, behold Membertou up and about, ready to live fifty years longer."

By early April, as the fish began their seasonal run, the situation for the French slowly improved. Remarkably, through all their troubles, no one died or even showed symptoms of scurvy. Then on May 22, in the half-light of evening, the *Grâce-de-Dieu* dropped anchor in front of the Habitation.

Artistic rendering of Jesuits on their way to North America

Clash of Secular and Spiritual Powers

The Jesuits stepped ashore at Port-Royal with the singular objective of establishing a mission to administer to the Amerindians, while Poutrincourt and Biencourt were preoccupied with establishing a colony and the trading necessary to sustain it. Clashes over priorities were inevitable.

The four-month voyage on the *Grâce-de-Dieu* had been beset with storms and icebergs "as big and as broad...as the Church of [Notre] Dame de Paris..." According to Father Biard, "We could rest neither day nor night...We fell over each other and against the baggage...cups were spilled over our beds and bowls in our laps, or a big wave demanded our plates." But whatever misgivings Biencourt may have had towards the "black robes," he had apparently treated the Fathers with respect, even allowing Biard to share his cabin. Remarkably, they had met Champlain who was heading to Quebec in late April.

Biencourt had stopped along the way to trade, including at a place called Port St.-Jean, which seems to have been near LaHave (Nova Scotia). During this stopover, Biard and Massé had their first encounter with Amerindians, in all probability Mi'kmaq, who declared themselves Christians, including a chief named Cacagous (possibly Ka'kau'j, meaning crow), who claimed to have been baptized in France. Biard was unimpressed, however, for they neither understood what it meant to be baptized nor what their Christian names were. When he asked how many wives he had, the chief replied that he had eight, seven of whom were with him, "pointing them out with...much pride, instead of an equal degree of shame," as Biard wrote later. But as Olive Dickason notes: "Observing the importance the French attached to their religion, the Amerindians [including the Mi'kmaq] reacted by assuming that participation in this ritual would cement their alliance with the Christians. When Biard and Énemond Massé arrived at Port-Royal in 1611, they found that the baptized Amerindians considered themselves allies of the French, 'already nearly Normans' [as they called the French]."

Soon after the arrival of the *Grâce-de-Dieu*, a group of Etchemins (probably Passamaquoddy) from the St. Croix area came to the Habitation to complain that a Captain La Coq had robbed them and killed one of their women. Poutrincourt, Biencourt, and Father Biard sailed to a port called Pierre Blanche, located near the mouth of the St. Croix River, to confront the interloper and to enforce Biencourt's authority as vice-admiral.

Although La Coq had departed, they found four ships, including one belonging to the Sieur de Mons, and another, owned by Pont-Gravé, who was not there, commanded by a Captain La Salle. Each of the captains recognized Biencourt's authority as vice-admiral and several even loaned Poutrincourt provisions. After pleadings from Father Biard, Poutrincourt agreed to allow him to go and find Pont-Gravé. The year before, Poutrincourt had imprisoned Pont-Gravé for an apparent misdeed toward an Amerindian woman (historical sources suggest, though not explicitly, that the woman was raped). But he had managed to escape and spent the winter with the Wolastoqiyik. Biard located Pont-Gravé and intervened on his behalf with Poutrincourt; a truce was eventually reached between the two rivals, after which Poutrincourt invited Biard to dine with him and La Salle.

During the gathering, Captain La Salle apparently insulted Biencourt by not showing him due deference as vice-admiral, so Biard again acted as a go-between. By now, however, both Poutrincourt and Biencourt felt that Biard was siding with their rivals. Poutrincourt was particularly annoyed at the priest's interference in what he considered civil matters, saying, according to a later *factum*, or statement of facts, "Father, I pray that you leave me to do my duty. I know it very well and hope to go straight to Paradise as well with my sword as you with your breviary. Show me the road to heaven; I will lead you well on earth." Poutrincourt and company arrived back at the Habitation in early June.

Father Biard was unimpressed with his and Father Massé's room, claiming that it was so small that "we can scarcely turn around when we have a table in it…[however] the other dwellings also, as is to be expected among new settlers, are by no means large or commodious." He also complained that "we have been obliged to take a servant to do the drudgery. We could not dispense with one without a great deal of anxiety and trouble." To his dismay, Biard also found the Habitation's chapel unsuited for religious services, and so Poutrincourt gave the priests "an entire quarter of his habitation" if they could roof it over and adapt it to their needs.

After several weeks at Port-Royal, Biard wrote a letter to his superiors in which he outlined his initial impressions about the Amerindians: "The nation is savage, wandering and full of bad habits; the people few and isolated. They are [wild], hunting the woods, ignorant, lawless and rude: they are wanderers with nothing to attach them to a place…they have bad habits, are extremely lazy, gluttonous, profane, treacherous, cruel in their revenge, and given up to all kinds of lawlessness, men and women alike." He did, however, make an exception for Membertou, whom he called "the greatest, most renowned...[Amerindian] that ever lived in the memory of man."

During a conversation with Chief Membertou, according to a translation by Biencourt, the chief gave Biard a witty answer when asked to recite 'Give us our daily bread' from the Lord's Prayer. Membertou apparently replied, "if I did not ask him for anything but bread, I would be without moose-meat or fish."

Poutrincourt readied the *Grâce-de-Dieu* for the return trip to France, with no profits having been made. While poor weather and his own precarious financial situation were the main reasons for this outcome, Poutrincourt chose instead to blame the Jesuits, as historian Elizabeth Jones writes: "Here were the new men insidiously intriguing their way in causing delays, and now wanting to 'have a finger in too many pies.'" Poutrincourt departed Port-Royal on June 11, with thirty-eight aboard, including Abbé Fléché, Sieurs Bertrand, Belot, and Jouy, and the workers who had spent the winter. Biencourt took charge of the Habitation and the Jesuits set about their missionary duties.

The Jesuits' main challenge was trying to understand the Mi'kmaw language, for as Biard noted, "it is no simple matter to draw out from the [Mi'kmaq and other Amerindians] the words that they know." The Mi'kmaq, for example, could readily understand concepts such as strong, good, red, and hard; but their language did not accommodate abstract terms such faith, hope, sacrament, baptism, and incarnation, since there were no equivalent Mi'kmaw expressions. To resolve this impasse, Biard decided to move the mission to the St. John River area where Pont-Gravé was still operating. Since Pont-Gravé had lived with the Amerindians, Biard felt that he would be a better translator than Biencourt, but the latter became furious on hearing of this plan. Biard later wrote that Biencourt took such offence that "we had to yield [to] him, to have peace." Biencourt apparently shared his father's deep distrust of the Jesuits, an attitude that was to cloud his judgement on more than one occasion.

In late August, Biencourt, accompanied by Father Biard, went to St. Croix Island, where he found a Captain Plâtrier, who had wintered there with his men—the first documented time Europeans had done so since 1604. In his capacity as vice-admiral, Biencourt intended to charge Plâtrier a tax on his furs; however, Plâtrier, who acknowledged Biencourt's authority, said that English fishermen, claiming ownership of the area, had stolen them.

Biencourt and company arrived back at the Habitation on September 8, where they found Membertou in the priests' room, gravely ill with dysentery. While apothecary Hébert brought food and medicine, the priests performed the tedious tasks of caring for the chief, especially keeping the fire going to ward off the almost unbearable stench of illness in the small room. When Membertou's wife and a daughter came to be with him, Biard asked Biencourt to relocate the chief to one of the empty rooms in the Habitation because "it was neither good nor quite seemly that there should be women in their cabin day and night." Instead, Biencourt moved Membertou to his wigwam located near the Habitation. With each passing day, however, his health diminished and at Biencourt's urging, the chief made a general confession to Father Biard.

While Membertou continued his funeral oration, a heated discussion between Biencourt and Biard unfolded over whether he should be interred in his people's secret burial place, as the chief had requested, or

Former Mi'kmaw grand chief Donald Marshall unveiling the Historic Sites and Monuments Board of Canada plaque commemorating Chief Membertou, 1985

be buried in consecrated ground. Upon assurances, however, that his followers would still visit the Habitation, the chief agreed to be buried in Christian ground. Membertou died on Sunday, September 18, 1611. The next day, following a mass in the chapel attended by members of his family, Membertou's body was taken, with "the men carrying arms, drums beating as in a funeral procession for captains," to the Port-Royal cemetery for burial. A large cross was set up over his grave, on which were hung his bow and arrows. Henceforth Membertou was called "the great Captain."

In early October, Biencourt, Father Biard, Louis Hébert, Charles de La Tour, several Amerindian guides, likely Mi'kmaq, and about twelve men, sailed towards the Saco River, Maine, to trade for food. First Biencourt crossed the Bay of Fundy to confront Pont-Gravé, who, along with a Captain Merveille and a number of Malouins, was wintering on an island in the St. John River. He intended to force Pont-Gravé to give him one-fifth of his furs. When Biencourt arrived, however, he only found a few of the Malouins; a tense standoff ensued. When Captain Merveille returned that evening he was met with a hostile reception from Biencourt's sentries. A heated exchange arose, and Merveille and three of the Malouins were soon bound with rope. The following afternoon, Pont-Gravé arrived and

Re-creation of Mi'kmaq playing the dice game *waltes*

a truce was soon reached between the two rivals. Captain Merveille even loaned Biencourt a ship, which he "took…with him, together with one of the [Malouins], who afterwards died at Port Royal."

Biencourt and company continued their voyage towards the Saco River. Along the way, they passed the abandoned remnants of Fort St. George, which the Plymouth Company had built four years earlier at the mouth of the Kennebec River. The next day, several Amerindians guided them up an offshoot of the river to meet with Etchemin chief Météourmite, whom they said would supply them with corn (Champlain and de Mons had met him during their voyage along the coast in the spring of 1605). The French, however, could not navigate the shallow waters and their guides had mysteriously disappeared. On their descent they met Météourmite, whose followers then guided them to their chief's encampment. While Météourmite and Biencourt held a parley, Father Biard was taken to the largest wigwam in the chief's apparently impressive headquarters, where there were almost eighty people. He administered to them and blessed their children; finally Biard felt that he was fulfilling his missionary duties.

In what was an early indication of how Amerindians came to view the French and English, Chief Météourmite spoke about how his people's encounter with the English differed with that of the French (recognizing that the comments were recorded by the French who were there). While they seem to have liked the Englishman John Popham, Elizabeth Jones writes that "the next captain, Raleigh Gilbert, proved so ferocious to the [Amerindians] that they took their revenge by killing eleven Englishmen." (Popham and Gilbert of the Plymouth Company had established the English settlement at the mouth of the Kennebec River in 1607.) Chief Météourmite, however, put the French at ease by saying that they were different and, as Biard later wrote, "saying that they loved us very much, because they knew we would not close our doors to the [Amerindians] as the English did, and that we would not drive them from our table with blows from a club, nor set our dogs upon them." Father Biard thought that Chief Météourmite was flattering them for his own purposes. Nonetheless, he was impressed, but perhaps a bit frustrated, with the chief's long-winded speech: "These people are, I believe, the greatest speech makers in the world; nothing can be done without speeches."

It was now early November and too late to carry on to Saco, so the French headed back towards Port-Royal. On the return voyage they sailed up the Penobscot River where they came across about three hundred Amerindians, eighty canoes, and eighteen wigwams. They met with Etchemin chief Bashabes, whom Biard was particularly taken with, and in a later report he seemed to question, if ever so slightly, his initial preconceived views about the Amerindians: "I confess we often see in these [Amerindians] natural and graceful qualities which will make anyone but a shameless person blush, when they compare them to the greater part of the French who come over here."

Still without food, Biencourt went to St. Croix Island where Captain Plâtrier lent them two barrels of peas and beans. The expedition arrived back at the Habitation on November 18, 1611, with no relief ship in sight and almost no provisions as winter began to close in.

Trading Post and Mission

In France, meanwhile, Poutrincourt had been unable to secure the funds to purchase supplies for Port-Royal. In desperation he approached Mme de Guercheville, who agreed to outfit a vessel provided she was made an equal partner in his enterprise. Poutrincourt insisted, however, that their contract affirm and protect his continued ownership of Port-Royal and the "adjacent lands as far as and as wide as they may extend." Mme de Guercheville, in turn, demanded to see his titles of ownership, but he excused himself saying that they were at Port-Royal.

Suspicious of Poutrincourt's response, Mme de Guercheville met with Sieur de Mons, who confirmed that Poutrincourt did indeed own only the immediate area of Port-Royal. De Mons then relinquished to her (he had lost his monopoly, but not his title as lieutenant general of Acadie) "all rights, deeds, and claims that he had, or ever had, in New France, derived from the gift made him by the late Henry the Great." King Louis XIII confirmed the grant, effectively giving her—meaning the Jesuits by proxy—title of all the lands of New France from, "the great river of Canada (St. Lawrence River) as far as Florida, excepting Port Royal, which was what Sieur de Poutrincourt possessed then, and nothing else." The Jesuits would later flatter themselves on this achievement, writing that by restricting Poutrincourt to Port-Royal he would be "locked up and confined as in a prison." Mme de Guercheville entrusted her funds to Jesuit Brother Gilbert Du Thet, who was to give them to the Dieppe merchant contracted to outfit a vessel. But somehow Poutrincourt managed to persuade the gullible Du Thet to give him a portion, which he then used to have another vessel readied by one Simon Imbert Sandrier.

Captain Nicolas L'Abbé the younger, Simon Imbert, and Brother Du Thet left Dieppe in late November of 1611 and arrived at the Habitation on January 23, 1612, where they found hunger and conflict. Food supplies had become so low that "There was given to each individual for the entire week only about ten ounces of bread, half a pound of lard, three bowls of peas or beans, and one of prunes." During their occasional visits, members of Membertou's family brought fresh game, at which time there was "great feasting and [laughter], and our people would begin to feel a little encouraged." Yet, for some unexplained reason the French appear to have been unable to hunt for their own game. Isolated in their Habitation, and "their dread of the season, when they considered the long duration of disagreeable months to be endured" the men turned on one another. Perhaps not surprisingly, the main conflict had involved Biencourt and the Jesuits.

Biencourt apparently felt that the fathers had not baptized enough Amerindians, while the priests had refused to perform baptisms without first providing instruction. Biard himself was also discouraged, as reflected in a report he made to his superiors in which he held out "little hope for the mission." Biencourt believed the Jesuits' lack of enthusiasm was undermining the colony and his leadership; as Elizabeth Jones notes: "He himself sensed the priests' doubts, and felt that he was being watched, weighed in the balance, and found wanting."

While the men were genuinely relieved to see the relief ship arrive, it brought only a small quantity of supplies, including some domestic animals that survived the crossing; for Father Massé said that Captain L'Abbé, "like a wise Noah in his ark, preserved species of animals, so they could propagate others in this land." Biencourt, however, was displeased to see yet another Jesuit, Brother Du Thet, disembark. But Poutrincourt's representative, Simon Imbert, was also on board and within a day Brother Du Thet and Imbert had begun to quarrel.

In short, Brother Du Thet claimed that Imbert had misappropriated, to Mme de Guercheville's loss, some of the food destined for the colony and so the Jesuits asked Biencourt to "discreetly" inquire about the supposedly missing provisions. Instead, Biencourt blurted out to Imbert that the Jesuits were accusing him of theft; he countered with the charge that Du Thet was a traitor for supposedly saying that it was good for Christendom that Henri IV had been killed. Biencourt decided that the accusation against Imbert was unfounded, but he also refused to issue affidavits and allow Brother Du Thet to go to France to defend himself. Fathers Biard and Massé protested by locking themselves in their room. Tensions increased further when they boarded the ship with the intention of leaving Port-Royal. Biencourt insisted that they return to shore, forgetting, or simply ignoring, that the Jesuits were his equal partners and could leave if they wished. When Father Massé finally disembarked, he bluntly told Biencourt that he did not recognize his position and that his own authority came from the king. He also informed Biencourt that he had been excommunicated. Following drawn-out negotiations, Biard finally agreed to disembark as well, provided Biencourt freed Captain L'Abbé, who had been imprisoned for allegedly "conspiring" with the priests.

Biencourt again revealed his contempt for the Jesuits in a letter to his father, Poutrincourt, in which, as Elizabeth Jones writes, Biencourt felt he had cause to congratulate himself on doing his duty: "'I have kept these Fathers from roaming around, as they wanted to do, until the King, their Provincial or General orders me to send them back. Also they might use some underhand means on the ship to have it go where they wish.'" Biencourt's prejudices and conspiracy-laden insecurities towards the Jesuits were also reflected in this same letter, which he concluded: "'I beg you, monsieur mon père, to waste no time in showing up the wickedness of these Jesuits and trust them as little as possible.'"

The turmoil was not isolated to Port-Royal. When the relief ship arrived back in France, it and the cargo were seized for payment of debts associated with the earlier outfitting of the vessel. Poutrincourt, meanwhile, was being assailed from all sides as he struggled to send additional supplies to Port-Royal. In fact, he became so distressed and anxious for the colonists that the situation "came near to ending him completely." But he recovered and continued lobbying for financial and material support.

Back at Port-Royal, relations between the Jesuits and Biencourt remained strained. However, after three months of tension and recriminations, the fathers decided to break the impasse. Each party listened to the other's complaints and interpretations of what had taken place (while Biard humbly apologized, Biencourt responded in a haughty tone, lecturing the priest on his duties). Nonetheless, reconciliation was finally achieved, with Biencourt even agreeing to allow Brother Du Thet to leave if he could find a ship that was willing to take him back to France.

The Jesuits resumed their missionary work by undertaking a comprehensive study of the Mi'kmaw language. Father Massé and the servant boy, Guillaume Crito, went to live with Membertou's son, baptized Louis, and his family for the summer. But the Frenchmen almost died from the experience. The food did not agree with them, and "they became thin, and lost their strength, color, and cheerfulness; their legs grew big, and heavy, and their minds were dulled, and a low fever set in." At one point Massé thought he was going blind. Although they recovered and returned to the Habitation, Massé appears to have made little progress in learning the Mi'kmaw language.

The year of 1612 had been disastrous for the Mi'kmaq as many fell ill and died from once-unknown diseases such as pleurisy and dysentery. Father Biard wrote that "[The Mi'kmaq] are astonished and often complain that since the French mingle with and carry on trade with them, they are dying fast and the population is thinning out....One by one the different coasts, according as they have begun to traffic with us, have been more reduced by disease....During this year alone [1612] sixty have died at Cape de la Hève, which is the greater part of those who lived there." Ethnologist Ruth Holmes Whitehead speculates that Chief Messamouet may have died in this epidemic, as his name never recurs in the historical record after this.

Across the Atlantic, events had once again taken a turn for the worse. Brother Du Thet had somehow made his way back to France, because in early October he had provided Mme de Guercheville with a detailed account of what had taken place, at least from the Jesuits' perspective. Moreover, he had arrived just as a ship was about to depart for Port-Royal. Poutrincourt and Mme de Guercheville had formed a joint venture; he had borrowed 750 livres from one Louis Beauxhoste against a bond and she had provided the same amount.

Outraged by what Brother Du Thet had told her, Mme de Guercheville decided to launch a new and much larger expedition—she and the Jesuits were going to establish a colony elsewhere. Upon hearing this, Poutrincourt commenced a complicated legal proceeding in an attempt to recover his investment. But before the matter could be resolved, an agent of Simon Lemaistre, a Rouen outfitter, had Poutrincourt arrested and imprisoned for failure to pay the bond, which Elizabeth Jones says Beauxhoste had conveyed to Lemaistre. After much pleading, Poutrincourt was freed; yet, only a week later another judge ordered him to pay the debt. Mysteriously, Poutrincourt found enough money to pay off his debt and to purchase supplies and outfit the *Grâce-de-Dieu*. With all the delays, however, it was too late in the season to send supplies to Port-Royal; he would have to wait until the spring of 1613.

Conflict on the Continent

On March 12, 1613, the *Jonas*, commanded by Mme de Guercheville's agent, René Le Coq de La Saussaye—who it seems wanted to establish an idyllic agricultural settlement in the "New World"—sailed from Honfleur with forty-eight on board, including Captain Charles Fleury, an interpreter, one Jean-Jacques Simon, and Jesuits Father Jacques Quentin and Brother Gilbert Du Thet. Nearly two months later the *Jonas* reached Cap de la Héue (Cape LaHave, Nova Scotia), where the passengers said mass and erected a cross on which were affixed Mme de Guercheville's coat of arms as a sign of having taken possession of the area in her name. They arrived at Port-Royal on May 16, where they found Louis Hébert, who was in charge, Fathers Biard and Massé, their servant Guillaume Crito, and one other man; Biencourt and the others were off fishing and trading for provisions. The queen's letters were presented and "these fathers withdrew their goods from the country, and left [a barrel of bread and bottels of wine] to this Hébert."

Partial view of the reconstructed 1607 Jamestown, Virginia

In the interval, a contract had been drawn up between Poutrincourt and La Rochelle merchants Macain and Georges, who had loaned him funds at a twenty-five per cent interest rate, and they were to be given all the furs from the return journey. The *Grâce-de-Dieu* was now heading for Port-Royal, having left France on May 5.

Around May 20, the *Jonas* sailed from Port-Royal bound for Kadesquit on the Penobscot River, Maine. By sheer happenstance, however, they came out of the fog near Mount Desert Island where they entered today's Frenchman Bay. They said mass and planted a cross, and named the place Saint-Sauveur. As the expedition's leaders squabbled about whether they should continue to Kadesquit, their original destination, smoke signals suddenly appeared from on shore. A party, which included Biard, was sent to investigate. Here they found several of Armouchiquois chief Asticou's followers who pleaded with Biard to go visit the chief, claiming that he was ill and feared dying without baptism. Biard and several others travelled by canoe the short distance to Asticou's base camp, only to discover that it was just a ploy to induce the French to stay—it worked. The *Jonas* was brought to the new location, which particularly impressed Biard, where they planted another cross and erected tents. Their plans, however, were soon interrupted when sails of a different kind appeared on the horizon.

In the early summer of 1613, Captain Samuel Argall—who as admiral of Virginia was empowered to expel all foreign intruders from English-claimed territory, particularly the Spanish who had known intentions of eliminating the English—had sailed from Jamestown for a group of islands at the mouth of the Kennebec River, which the English used as a summer fishing base. During the voyage, however, strong winds, thick fog, and the current forced his frigate, the *Treasurer*, off course. When the weather cleared on July 2, Argall and his crew of sixty men found themselves near Mount Desert Island.

Several Amerindians, thinking the ship was French, sailed out to greet the English. From their gestures and use of the expression "Normandia," Argall concluded that there were likely French nearby.[4] Guided by one of the Amerindians, the English sailed into Frenchman Bay where they

---

[4] Historian Austin Squires says that the English knew that French colonization was continuing near or in English-claimed territory, which was confirmed in 1611 when bad weather forced the *Grâce-de-Dieu*, with Biencourt and Fathers Biard and Massé on board, to put in at the Isle of Wight while on its way to Port-Royal.

found the *Jonas*. Argall's men prepared for a fight as the *Treasurer*, with the banners of England flying, and "three trumpets and two drums making a horrible [noise]..." bore down on the *Jonas*.

Captain Fleury, Brother Du Thet, and a few others rushed aboard the *Jonas*, but La Saussaye kept most of the men on shore. The English easily captured the French vessel; six French were wounded, including Brother Du Thet, who died the next day. Meanwhile, according to Biard, La Saussaye and his men took refuge in the woods,

[as Argall] set his soldiers to plundering, and in this the whole afternoon was consumed.

From shore we looked on at the pillage of our property: for the English had left us on shore while they remained on the water where they joined our vessels to theirs, for we had two, [the Jonas*] and a barque...We were reduced to a pitiful state, but this was not the end. The next day they came on shore, and robbed us also of what we had there.*

Argall also confiscated the royal commission from La Saussaye's sea chest. When he reappeared, La Saussaye could not produce his documents and so Argall pretended to treat the French as pirates. What was now to become of the French?

Father Biard says that Amerindians (possibly some of Chief Asticou's followers) came to them at night and offered "us their canoes and their help to take us anywhere we wished to go." They also offered to take in the French until the next year when vessels would be on the coast, "and promising to feed us during the Winter, and showing a great deal of sympathy for us...and in that way we should be able to go back to our country without falling into the hands of the wicked Ingreés, as they called the English."

La Saussaye and Argall eventually reached acceptable terms, whereby the latter would take the *Jonas* and fifteen men, including Nicolas de La Mothe (La Saussaye's lieutenant), Captain Fleury, three workmen (who agreed to work in Virginia for a year), Fathers Biard and Quentin, and their servant, Guillaume Crito. The remaining fifteen, including La Saussaye and Father Massé, were to be set adrift in an open boat.

Those in the open boat had almost no sailing experience, but were intercepted by Bailleau, who, with fourteen others, had managed to evade the English. Sailors were divided between the two boats and they sailed off together. At port Fourchu (Yarmouth, Nova Scotia) they met Membertou's son, Louis—now it seems a chief in his own right—who "made *Tabagie* (feast) for them all with Moose Meat, which was a great blessing to them." Some Mi'kmaq at Port Mouton—including the younger son of Panoniac, whose killing in 1606 had led to Membertou's war against the Armouchiquois—gave them sea biscuits and, ironically, as Father Biard would later write, "Behold the world turned upside down [as] the [Amerindians] freely furnish[ed] bread to the French." The Mi'kmaq also told them that there were two ships near Kjipuktuk (the Mi'kmaw name for today's Halifax), one of which belonged to Robert Pont-Gravé. After a terrifying return voyage, they arrived safely at Saint-Malo, France in mid-October.

Argall, meanwhile, had returned to Jamestown, Virginia, where he reported to the deputy governor, Sir Thomas Dale, who initially wanted to hang the French "pirates." After due deliberation, the council in Virginia, which included Argall, directed him to sail north and to plunder all French ships and destroy all settlements as far as Cape Breton. He sailed from Jamestown with some of the French prisoners, who would be allowed to return to France, and three ships: a small unnamed vessel taken from Saint-Sauveur, the *Treasurer* with Captain Fleury and four other Frenchmen on board, and the captured *Jonas*, on which were Fathers Biard and Quentin, and their servant, Guillaume Crito.

Landing first at Saint-Sauveur, the English destroyed what remained of the settlement, tore down the French cross and replaced it with one bearing the name of the king of England. They then sailed to St. Croix Island, where they burned the remnants of de Mons' 1604 settlement and took a supply of salt stored there by French fishermen. Argall then crossed the Bay of Fundy, entering Port-Royal on October 31 under the cover of darkness and anchored out of sight of the Habitation. Biard claimed that the English had captured a local Amerindian chief who then guided them to Port-Royal, but Poutrincourt later placed the blame solely on Biard. Another probable scenario, however, was that Argall was guided by the charts that he had taken from the *Jonas* when he seized it while at Mount Desert Island. However the English got there, the surprise was complete.

The next morning, Argall and his men found the Habitation empty—Biencourt and some men were away visiting the Mi'kmaq, while the others were harvesting wheat upriver. The *Grâce-de-Dieu* sent by Poutrincourt had arrived during the summer, so the stores were likely not empty. There were also cattle, horses, and hogs in adjacent fields and pens.

After plundering the rooms, the English raiders stripped the buildings of all useful materials, right down to the door hinges. Then they set the

Habitation on fire; the flames quickly engulfed the wooden structure as plumes of thick black smoke rose skyward. Within two hours the settlement was reduced to a smouldering heap of ashes. The rampage continued as Argall's men, using a pick and chisel, methodically effaced the fleur-de-lys and "the names of sieur de Mon[s] and other Captains" from a boulder located nearby. They butchered some of the livestock and loaded other animals, including horses, onto the ships, and then sailed upriver

The coat of arms of King Henri IV of France and Navarre, and those of (left) Pierre Dugua, Sieur de Mons and Jean de Biencourt de Poutrincourt et de Saint-Just. Similar standards were placed above the entrance to the original Habiation to welcome Poutrincourt and crew back from their voyage to Cape Cod on November 14, 1606.

to the wheat fields. Biencourt's men fled to higher ground as the English approached. The French shouted abuses at Biard and called for Argall to kill the Jesuit as his men collected some wheat and then burned the rest. Only the water-mill and several outbuildings were spared because the low tide prevented the attackers from reaching them.

Biencourt returned just as the English were about to sail from Port-Royal. He met with Argall, who apparently credited the Jesuits with causing the governor of Virginia to order the attack. Biencourt then launched into a ferocious and bitter condemnation of Biard during which Biencourt demanded that he be handed over, but Argall refused. An anonymous English authority claimed (unconfirmed by other sources) that Biencourt offered to join the English if permitted to remain at Port-Royal under English protection, which Argall turned down.

Argall sailed from Port-Royal around November 13, satisfied that he had proclaimed English sovereignty of the area, while the French were left to their devices. Shortly after the Virginian fleet departed, however, a fierce storm scattered the ships; the smallest vessel was never heard from again. Argall's *Treasurer* made it back to Jamestown about three weeks later. For his exploits, a contemporary wrote that "Captain Argall whose indevors in this action intitled him most worthy." The *Jonas*, meanwhile, with Lieutenant Turner in command and with Fathers Biard and Quentin, and Guillaume Crito on board, was blown off course; a decision was taken to steer a course east towards the Portuguese Azores. During the long voyage they "killed all the horses that had been taken at Port Royal, which they ate, in lieu of provisions." Around mid-February of 1614, they reached Milford Haven, Wales. In late April, Fathers Biard and Quentin, and Guillaume Crito finally reached France, their rescue having been obtained by the French ambassador to England.

Yet, the history of Port-Royal—the area surrounding today's Annapolis Basin—did not end with the destruction of the French Habitation. The competition between France and England to establish permanent colonies set the stage for the struggle for supremacy in North America that would engulf the imperial powers and the Mi'kmaq and other Amerindians over the next 150 years.

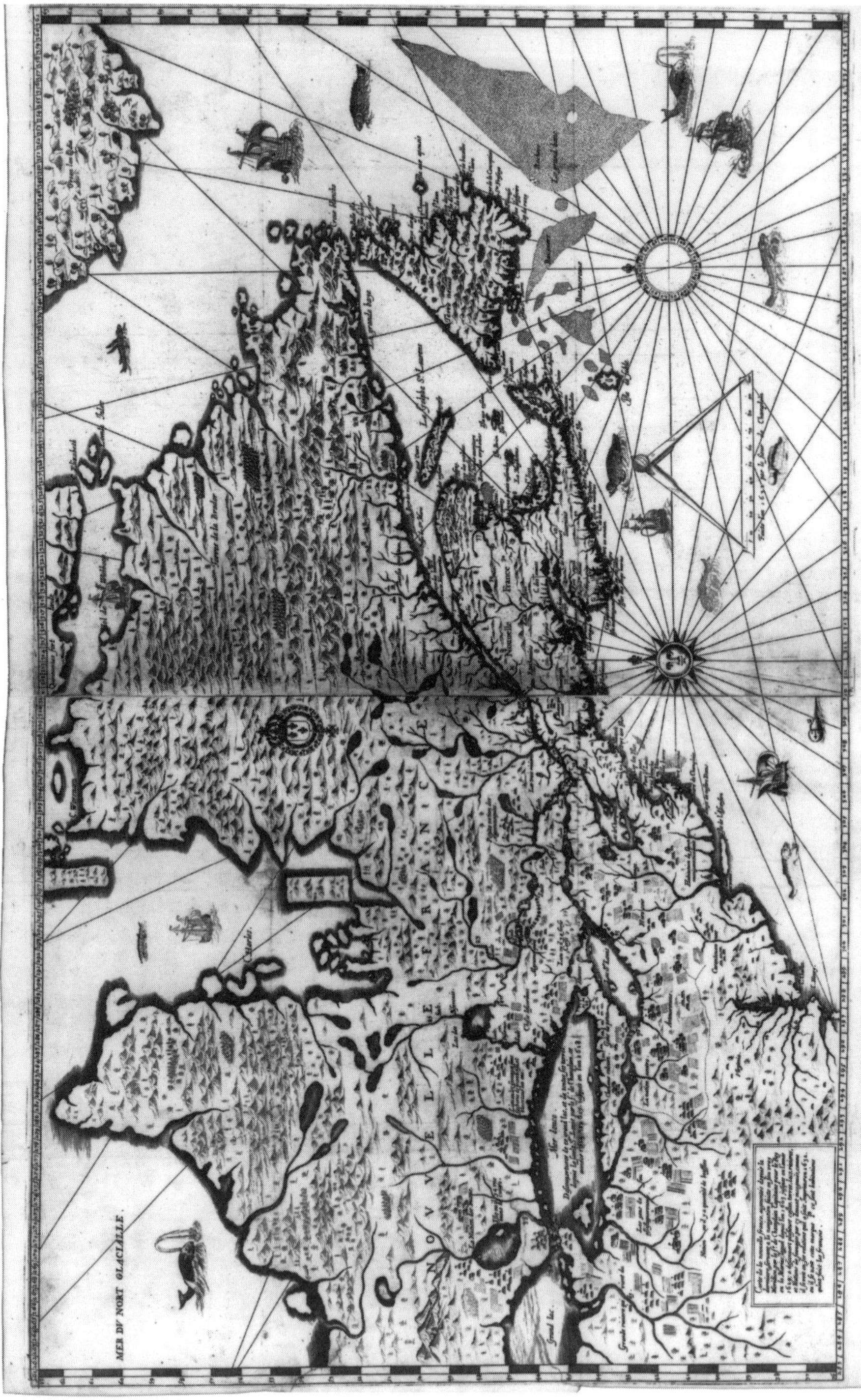
MER DV NORT GLACIALLE

EPILOGUE

Continuing French Presence

Published in 1632, three years before his death, this map by Champlain is amazingly accurate. In just thirty years, Champlain himself would, almost singlehandedly, establish the essential geography of Canada from Newfoundland to the Great Lakes. The map also indicates the areas where the different Amerindian societies of the era lived.

DESPITE THE ENORMOUS contribution Sieur de Mons made to the exploitation and development of Canada during its foundation stage, he has received little recognition. For much of the past four hundred years, de Mons was overshadowed by Samuel de Champlain, even though de Mons was the one, as the principal backer, who made possible much of what Champlain achieved both in Acadie and Canada (Quebec). He played a central role in making the Atlantic region better known to Europeans through the precise mapping of Acadie, Quebec, and beyond that Champlain subsequently produced. As historian George MacBeath writes, "The energetic direction, support, and encouragement de [Mons] gave to exploration, which was subsequently reported in the writings of Champlain and Lescarbot, represents a contribution of inestimable value." Sieur de Mons' contributions ultimately led to a permanent French presence in northeastern North America.

The Argall attack on Port-Royal in 1613 was the opening salvo of what would become a century-and-a-half–long continental struggle between England and France. The French continued to maintain a presence in the years that followed, one which of course remains an important part of the Canadian identity.

In the spring of 1614, Poutrincourt returned to Port-Royal, with Louis Hébert and David Lomeron, nephew to one of his merchant partners, to find his Habitation destroyed. His son, Biencourt, Charles de La Tour and the others had spent the winter with the Mi'kmaq but were near to starvation. After ten years of effort, Poutrincourt left Port-Royal dejected and was to never return. He deeded his holdings to his son, and the following year was killed during the civil uprisings in France.

Biencourt, Charles de La Tour, his father Claude, and a few others stayed on at Port-Royal. They supplied their agent David Lomeron with furs and fish, and maintained their close ties with the Mi'kmaq and other Amerindians. As well, either Biencourt or Charles de La Tour may have built a fort next to the ruins of the Port-Royal Habitation. Sometime in 1617-18 Biencourt shifted his base from Port-Royal to Cape Sable. According to historian Brenda Dunn, Claude de La Tour "apparently [engaged] in the fur trade and fishery in the Penobscot area and [built] a fort at Pentagouet (now Castine, Maine) in the 1620s." She also says that when Biencourt died in 1623, he left his territory and rights in Acadie to his brother, Jacques de Biencourt, living in France, and direction of the settlement to his friend, Charles de La Tour.

Charles de La Tour built a fort at Cape Sable, which was the last remaining French presence in Acadie. He carried on a sizable fur trade, farmed, and married a Mi'kmaw woman with whom he had three daughters. La Tour would later bring families from France to settle in Acadie. By the late 1620s, however, Acadie was to witness the arrival of yet another group with claims to the territory.

In 1629, a group of Scottish setters built a fort at the confluence of what are now the Annapolis and Allain Rivers, near the spot where the French had planted their wheat between 1605 and 1613. The Scots, who continued to call the area Port Royal, only stayed three years. Vestiges of the Scots' fort form part of today's Fort Anne. Their legacy also continues through the name their Latin charter gave the colony: namely Nova Scotia, meaning New Scotland. The coat of arms granted to Sir William Alexander by Charles I in 1625 still serve as the province's coat of arms and its shield inspired the design of the present-day Nova Scotia flag.

Port-Royal was handed back to the French under the Treaty of Saint-Germain-en-Laye in 1632, and for a few years in the 1630s, LaHave was the principal French settlement, under the leadership of Isaac de Razilly. Shortly after Razilly's death in 1636, its new leader, Charles de Menou d'Aulnay, and most of the settlers relocated to Port-Royal (a name they continued to use), establishing themselves where the Scots had placed their fort.

In the 1630s, the first French families began to settle in Acadie. The focus of the initial colonizing phase between 1604 and 13 had been on the fur trade and involved only males. The migration of families from France marked a dramatic shift. As of 1650, there were approximately fifty families, around four hundred inhabitants, of European origin in the region. These families formed the foundation for the development of the Acadian people.

Creation of a National Historic Site

For over three centuries, the presumed site of the 1605 Port-Royal Habitation remained relatively undisturbed. It was not until 1911 that any serious attempt was made to identify the original location, when Dr. William F. Ganong investigated and marked what he believed was the position of the original Habitation. In 1924, the Historic Sites and Monuments Board of Canada erected a plaque commemorating the national significance of the site.

Gradually, the idea of reconstructing the Habitation took hold. The project was conceived and spearheaded by Harriette Taber Richardson, an American from Cambridge, Massachusetts. Since 1923, she had spent her summers in the area and was a dedicated student of its history. She proposed that the descendants of the New Englanders and Virginians who had destroyed the original in 1613 undertake the reconstruction of the Habitation. L. M. Fortier, honorary superintendent of Fort Anne National Historic Park, and Lieutenant-Colonel E. K. Eaton were keen supporters, as was the Historical Association of Annapolis Royal of which Mr. Fortier was president.

In 1930, Richardson organized the Associates of Port Royal to raise the then considerable sum of ten thousand dollars, which was to be presented

L. M. Fortier and Harriette Taber Richardson, 1931

"as a gift of goodwill to the Canadian Government for the rebuilding of the Habitation." The Historical Association of Annapolis Royal agreed to acquire the land, undertake the reconstruction, and provide for its maintenance. It was also hoped that this initiative would foster an exchange of ideas among those with an interest in early European life in both Canada and the United States, and even in France and England.

The building fund accumulated a goodly sum before the economic depression of the 1930s stopped the fund-raising drive. Although the Great Depression curtailed her initial efforts, Richardson, and others, kept the initative alive. Meanwhile, the Historical Association of Annapolis Royal acquired the necessary lands, but it was not until 1938 that the property that is the assumed site of the Habitation came up for sale. The province of Nova Scotia then purchased the property on behalf of the

Workers reconstructing the Port-Royal Habitation in 1938-39
[below] Tradesmen producing hand-made shingles for the reconstructed Habitation

Official opening of the reconstructed Port-Royal Habitation, July 4, 1941

Canadian government. Based on a survey by the National Parks Branch, the Government of Canada agreed to undertake its first reconstruction of a historic site. The Associates of Port Royal provided the services of C.C. Pinckney of Boston to do the archaeological investigations. He had done similar work at Colonial Williamsburg and at George Washington's Mount Vernon estate.

Work on the site began in September of 1938 and continued for about six weeks when activities stopped for the winter. During the following months, architectural and historical research was undertaken in support of developing the detailed construction drawings for the buildings. Charles W. Jefferys, the well-known Canadian illustrator and scholar, played an instrumental role in the project as one of several consultants. He also produced a series of detailed illustrations depicting daily life and drawings of the period furnishings at the Habitation in the early 1600s.

Based on the on-site findings, it was determined that "ample evidence had been found to enable building operations to proceed with confidence." (Present-day archaeologists have re-examined the evidence and have concluded that there was no conclusive proof that the reconstruction was re-built on the exact location of the original Habitation.)

Three hundred and twenty-eight years after the destruction of the original, the reconstructed Habitation was officially opened on July 4, 1941. Harriette Taber Richardson continued to take an active interest in the site until her death in 1951; as well, the Historical Association of Annapolis Royal continues its support of and interest in the site.

History Brought to Life

The compact design of the Habitation allows you to wander from room to room at a leisurely pace, during which you can discover the dramatic story of the French and Mi'kmaq, and other Amerindian peoples, in the early 1600s. Knowledgeable costumed interpreters have a wealth of information which, coupled with period demonstrations, help create a feeling for what it may have been like at the original Port-Royal Habitation. So what is there to see and do there?

Aerial view of Port-Royal National Historic Site of Canada

Period animator Wayne Melanson interpreting a gentleman at the Port-Royal Habitation

[below left] Period animator Joël Doucet working in a re-created garden at the Port-Royal Habitation

[below] Historical guide Judy Pearson, whose Mi'kmaw ancestors befriended the French at the original Port-Royal Habitation

Above the entrance to the Habitation are the coats of arms of Henri IV, King of France and Navarre, and of the Sieurs de Mons and de Poutrincourt. The covered gate opens into a central courtyard surrounded by the working and living areas. The Habitation's design, such as the steeply pitched roofs, is representative of Normandy-style architecture of the early 1600s.

The blacksmith played an important role at the original Habitation because in the forge he fabricated the hardware needed to build and maintain the settlement. If required, he could also produce the all-important metal goods used for trading with the Mi'kmaq and other Amerindians. Many of the tools on display date back to the early 1600s.

Next door to the forge is the kitchen. It was here that the daily meals and those for the Order of Good Cheer would have been prepared. A large fireplace with a turnspit for cooking is centrally located in the room. Typical examples of the pots, pans, and utensils that were used to prepare the food are on display. You can also get a close-up look at the wall construction, which is known as *en colombage*. On the back of the kitchen fireplace is the bake oven where a constant supply of bread was baked. From here, one enters the common room, where it is believed the approximately fifteen gentlemen who sat at Poutrincourt's table held the Order of Good Cheer during the winter of 1606-07.

Centrally located in this spacious room is the well-arranged large table with its pewter table settings, which allow you to imagine what it may have been like when the French, along with their Amerindian guests, such as Mi'kmaw chief Membertou, gathered for the Order of Good Cheer feasts. Along with plenty of wine and bread, the participants enjoyed delicacies such as fricasseed beaver tail and boiled moose nose.

Next door to the common room is the plainly built two-storey artisans' (workers) quarters, where it is believed the joiners, carpenters, masons, stonecutters, workers in iron and other workers lived. The foot-powered spring pole lathe, a modern-day reproduction, found in this room can be used to turn wood for many objects from spindles to goblets and candlesticks. An interpreter may demonstrate how it works. On display are examples of the types of tools used at the Habitation in the early 1600s. The men's sleeping area is located on the second floor. Bunk beds with straw mattresses and wool blankets bring to mind the sparse lodgings. Some of the mattresses are on the floor since the place could get quite crowded, especially when relief ships were in port. It is believed that the sick, such

View of the kitchen

Period animator Joël Doucet operating a foot-powered spring pole lathe

as those who suffered from scurvy, slept in the two small enclosed spaces next to the chimney.

From the workers' quarters, you can visit the simply arranged chapel, which is followed by what are believed to have been the gentlemen's rooms. Each is furnished with bunk beds and reproduction period furnishings. It is thought that there were usually two to four gentlemen per room. When strolling from room to room, one has the impression that the men have just left and are about to return at any moment.

One of the rooms brings to mind the apothecary, such as Louis Hébert, who may have occupied it in the original Habitation. One can imagine Hébert making various remedies by grinding herbs, examples of which hang from the rafters, in his mortar and pestle. The jars in the cabinet contain some of the medicines that were typically used to treat the sick in the early 1600s. Ask the interpreters to explain the various herbs and remedies, including those the French acquired from the Mi'kmaq. In another room, you can imagine poet-writer Marc Lescarbot sitting at a table in his study, as he called his room, reading or writing about daily life at Port-Royal.

A dwelling such as the one where apothecary Louis Hébert may have lived.

At the end of the row of gentlemen's rooms is what is commonly called the governor's house.

This is a well-built and furnished house as befits the leader's role in the colony. Above the large fireplace mantle are the coats of arms of Sieurs de Mons and de Poutrincourt as well as the French fleur-de-lis. Picture Sieur de Mons and Samuel de Champlain sitting in the leather-covered chairs in front of the fireplace discussing their plans for the next exploratory voyage. Take a look at the finely decorated smoked moose hide; Mi'kmaw elders wore similar painted hides. In fact, the French admired their work so much they used these hides as murals or tapestries. The window in the upstairs bedroom provides a lovely view of the central courtyard.

The fur trade was the economic lifeline of the colony and so it is not surprising that a large part of the original Habitation was dedicated to this critical activity. The Mi'kmaq and other Amerindians brought their pelts to the trading room, which they exchanged for the European trade goods displayed behind the counter. Attached to the trading room is a large storeroom where the furs were baled and stockpiled before being shipped to France. Underneath the storeroom floor is the wine cellar. A sail loft occupies the second floor of the storeroom.

Other areas to investigate include the cannon platform and palisade. Both provide spectacular views of the Annapolis River and basin beyond. From these vantage points one can certainly appreciate why Champlain named the area Port-Royal. There are a number of Historic Sites and Monuments Board of Canada plaques, including one commemorating the 375th anniversary of the baptism of Chief Membertou and his family into the Catholic faith in 1610, and another commemorating Harriette Taber Richardson for her tireless dedication to having the Habitation reconstructed in 1938-39.

Bibliography

Primary Sources

Campeau, Lucien, SI (ed.). *Monumenta Novae Franciae, vol. I : La Première Mission d'Acadie, 1602-1616*. Québec: Les Presses de l'Université Laval, 1967.

Champlain, Samuel. *The Works of Samuel de Champlain* (vol. 1, 1613 ed., edited by Henry P. Biggar). Toronto: Champlain Society, 1922-36 (Reprinted ed., Toronto: University of Toronto Press, 1971.)

——————————.*The Voyages of Samuel de Champlain, 1604-1616* (vol.1, 1632 ed., in *Trail Makers of Canada*, edited by Edward Gaylord Bourne). Toronto: The Courier Press, Ltd., 1911.

Harris, Kenneth D. "Restoration of the Habitation of Port Royal, N.S." *Journal of the Royal Architectural Institute of Canada*. Toronto, c. 1941.

Jefferys, C. W. "The Reconstruction of the Port Royal Habitation of 1605-13." *The Canadian Historical Review*. Toronto, December 1939.

Lescarbot, Marc. *Histoire de la Nouvelle France*. vols. 1-3. Toronto: Champlain Society, 1907-14. (Based on the 3rd ed., 1618; first published 1609.)

——————————. *Nova Francia: A Description of Acadia, 1606*. London: Harper & Brothers, 1928.

———. *Relation de la dernière de ce qui s'est passé au voyage du Sieur de Poutrincourt en la Nouvelle France depuis 20 mois ença*. Paris: Librairie Gabriel Enault, 1929. (First published 1612.)

Le Blant, Robert and René Baudry. *Nouveaux documents sur Champlain et son époque, 1560-1622*. Ottawa: Public Archives of Canada, 1967.

Morse, William Inglis (ed.). *Pierre Du Gua Sieur De Monts, Records: Colonial and "Saintongeois."* London: Bernard Quartitch Ltd., 1939.

Thwaites, Ruben Gold (ed.). *Jesuit Relations and Allied Documents*, vols. 1-4. Cleveland: Burrows Brothers Co., 1896-1901.

Secondary Sources

Armstrong, Joe. C.W. *Champlain*. Toronto: MacMillan of Canada, 1987.

Bourque, Bruce J. "Ethnicity on the Maritime Peninsula: 1600–1759," in *Journal of the American Society for Ethnohistory*, vol. 36, no.3, 1989.

Brown, George W. (ed.). *Dictionary of Canadian Biography, 1000-1700*, vol. I. Toronto: University of Toronto Press, 1966.

Christmas, Peter. "Micmac Aboriginal Life." Nd.

Dickason, Olive P. *Canada's First Nations: A History of Founding Peoples from Earliest Times*. Toronto: McClelland & Stewart Inc., 1992.

———. *The Myth of the Savage and the Beginnings of French Colonialism in the Americas*. Edmonton: University of Alberta Press, 1984.

Dunn, Brenda. A *History of Port-Royal / Annapolis Royal, 1605-1800*. Halifax: Nimbus Publishing Ltd., 2004.

Francis, Douglas R. (et al.). *Origins, Canadian History to Confederation*. Toronto: Harcourt Canada, 2000.

Ganong, Dr. William Francis. *Champlain's Island: Ste. Croix (Dochet)*. Saint John: New Brunswick Museum, reprinted 2004.

Hatch, Charles E. Jr. *The First Seventeen Years: Virginia, 1607-1624*. Charlottesville: University Press of Virginia, 1985.

Jaenen, Cornelius J. "The French Relationship with the Native Peoples of New France and Acadia." Ottawa: Indian and Northern Affairs, 1984.

Johnston, A.J.B. and W.P. Kerr. *Grand Pré: Heart of Acadie*. Halifax: Nimbus Publishing Ltd., 2004.

Jones, Elizabeth. *Gentlemen and Jesuits: Quest for Glory and Adventure in the Early Days of New France*. Toronto: University of Toronto Press, 1986.

Murdock, Beamish. *History of Nova Scotia or Acadie*, vol. I. Halifax: James Barnes, 1865.

Parkman, Francis. *Pioneers of France in the New World*, vol. 2. Toronto: George N. Morang & Co. Ltd., 1897.

Paul, Daniel. *We Were Not the Savages: A Micmac Perspective on the Collision of European and Aboriginal Civilization*. Halifax: Nimbus Publishing, 1993.

Ross, Sally and Alphonse J. Deveau. *The Acadians of Nova Scotia, Past and Present*. Halifax: Nimbus Publishing Ltd., 1992.

Société du Musée de Royan. *Naissance de la Nouvelle-France, Pierre Dugua de Mons*. Royan: Gatignol & Fils, 2000.

Soctomah, Donald. "The Passamaquoddy and French Connection: A 400 Year Relationship—St. Croix Island." 2004.

Whitehead, Ruth Holmes. *Elitekey: Micmac Material Culture from 1600 AD to the Present*. Halifax: Nova Scotia Museum, 1980.

—————————. *The Old Man Told Us: Excerpts from Micmac History 1500–1950*. Halifax: Nimbus Publishing Ltd., 1991.

Whitehead, Ruth Holmes and Harold McGee. *The Micmac: How Their Ancestors Lived Five Hundred Years Ago*. Halifax: Nimbus Publishing Ltd., 1983.

Image Sources

Amman, J. and Sachs, H., *Book of Trades*: 10

Bibliothèque national de France: 4

Canadian Museum of Civilization:
   Illustration by Francis Back, photo by Harry Foster (No. S97-9646): 42, (No. 989.56.10): 47

Kerr, W. P.: iii, 45 (bottom), 73, 80

Killiam, Dick:
   Front Cover, i, 93

Library and Archives Canada:
   9, 12 (both), 16, 22, 34, 48; C.W. Jefferys: 50; Montcornet: 54 (top); C.W. Jefferys: 56, 62, 69, 86

McCord Museum of Canadian History, Montreal:
   W. G. R. Hind (No. 1441): 15

Mi'kmaq Association for Cultural Studies/Learning Resources and Technology, NS Dept of Education: 14 (bottom), 35, 36, 45 (top), 52, 74

Native Council of Nova Scotia, Micmac language program: 14 (top)

Parks Canada: v; Dale Wilson: 7, 18, 33, 90, 92, 96, 98; Brian Townsend: 84, 94 (all), 97; C. W. Jefferys: 38, 43 (both), 44, 54 (bottom), 57, 66; Landmark Design: 53; R. Peck: 91 (both); Susan Tooke: 37 (both)

Rickett, Bruce: 59

U.S. National Park Service, Francis Back: 20, 21 (both), 24, 27

Index

Acadie 1, 5, 8, 11, 12, 16, 32, 33, 35, 40, 49, 58, 59, 61, 63, 64, 65, 67, 68, 76, 87, 88, 89, 101, 103
Alexander, Sir William 89
Antons, Sieur des 28
Ardamin, François 46
Argall, Samuel, captain 81-85
Asticou, Chief 64, 81, 82
Aubry, Nicolas 6, 23, 25
Bailleul, Israel 30, 82, 83
Bashabes, Chief 25, 76
Beauxhoste, Louis 79
Biard, Pierre, father 36, 68, 70, 71, 72, 73, 74, 75, 76, 77, 78, 79, 80, 81, 82, 83, 85
Biencourt, Jacques de 88
Biencourt de Poutrincourt et de Saint-Just, Jean 5, 46, 47, 49, 50, 51, 52, 55, 57, 58, 59, 60, 61, 64, 65, 67, 68, 69, 70, 71, 72, 76, 77, 78, 79, 81, 83, 88
Biencourt de Saint-Just, Charles de 46, 65, 67, 68, 70, 71, 72, 73, 74, 75, 76, 77, 78, 80, 83, 85
Boulay, Sieur du 6, 22, 33, 46
Bresson, Oliver 45
Cabahis, Chief 25, 26
Cacagous, Chief 70
Cartier, Jacques 28, 36
Champdoré, Pierre 6, 20, 22, 23, 32, 39, 40, 41, 49, 60, 64
Champlain, Samuel de 2, 5, 8, 12, 16, 17, 19, 23, 24, 25, 26, 28, 29, 30, 31, 32, 34, 35, 38, 39, 49, 50, 53, 55, 57, 60, 61, 63, 64, 70, 75, 87, 99, 101, 102

Chaste, Aymar de 7, 11
Chauvin, Pierre de 7
Chevalier, Captain 59, 60
Coman, Louis 6
Coton, Pierre, father 64, 65
Cramolet, Pierre 6, 30, 40
Crito, Guillaume 79, 80, 82, 83, 85
d'Entragues, Henriette, Marquise de Vernueil 68
Dale, Sir Thomas 83
Desbry, Claude 45
Deschamps, Guillaume 30, 39
de Coste, Mathieu 32, 33, 34
de La Mothe, Nicolas 82
de Mons, Sieur (Pierre Dugua) 1, 5, 6, 7, 8, 11, 12, 15, 16, 17, 19, 20, 21, 22, 23, 24, 25, 28, 29, 30, 32, 33, 40, 41, 42, 46, 47, 49, 52, 59, 61, 63, 64, 71, 75, 76, 83, 84, 87, 88, 95, 99, 103
de Pons, Antoinette, Marquise de Guercheville 65, 68, 76, 77, 79, 80
de Sourdis, Mme 68
Doucet, Joël 94, 97
Dugua, Pierre. *See* de Mons, Sieur (Pierre Dugua)
Duval, Jean 45, 51
Du Glas, Guillaume 6, 23
Du Jardin 68
Du Quesne 68
Du Thet, Gilbert, brother 76, 77, 78, 79, 80, 82
Eaton, E. K. 89
Esnault, Antoine 45
Fey, Louis 45

Fléché, Jessé, abbé 65, 67, 72
Fleury, Charles, captain 80, 82, 83
Fortier, L. M. 89, 90
Fougeray de Vitré, Sieur de 6, 32, 49
Foulques, Captain 6, 23, 25, 40
Ganong, Dr. William F. 89, 102
Georges 81
Gilbert, Raleigh 75
Gravé Du Pont, François 6, 7, 8, 12, 17, 23, 28, 31, 32, 39, 40, 41, 42, 46, 49, 61, 63
Gravé Du Pont, Robert. *See* Pont-Gravé, Robert
Guitard, François 45, 46
Hanin, Jean 45
Hay, Daniel 45
Hébert, Louis 46, 49, 52, 61, 65, 73, 74, 80
Henri IV 5, 7, 11, 13, 25, 59, 61, 63, 64, 65, 67, 77, 84, 95
Husson, Toussaint 45
Imbert, Simon 77
Jabart, Husson 45
James I 61
Jefferys, Charles W. 92, 101, 104
L'Abbé, Nicolas, captain 77, 78
La Cadie. *See* Acadie
La Coq, Captain 70, 71
La Roche, Marquis de 7, 28
La Salle, Captain 71
La Saussaye. *See* Le Coq de La Saussaye
Lemaistre, Simon 79
Le Coq de La Saussaye, René 80, 82
Lomeron, David 88
Louis XIII 76
Macain 81
Marchin, Chief 29, 30, 49, 60
Marshall, Donald, chief 73
Massé, Énemond, father 64, 65, 68, 70, 71, 77, 78, 79, 80, 82
Melanson, Wayne 94
Membertou, Chief 1, 36, 37, 40, 41, 42, 53, 57, 58, 60, 64, 67, 68, 69, 72, 73, 77, 79, 82, 95, 99

Menou d'Aulnay, Charles de 89
Merveille, Captain 74
Messamouet, Chief 16, 24, 49, 79
Météourmite, Chief 29, 75
Morel, Captain 6, 12
Onemechin, Chief 49, 60, 64
Order of Good Cheer 1, 57, 58, 95
Ouagimou, Chief 52, 60, 64
Panoniac 29, 52, 53, 60, 83
Pearson, Judy 94
Pinckney, C. C. 92
Plâtrier, Captain 72, 76
Pont-Gravé, Robert 46, 49, 51, 52, 71, 72, 74, 83
Popham, John 75
Poutrincourt. *See* Biencourt de Poutrincourt et de Saint-Just
Pussot, Jean 45
Quentin, Jacques, father 80, 82, 83, 85
Ralleau, Jean 5, 17, 64
Razilly, Isaac de 89
Richardson, Harriette Taber 89, 90, 93, 99
Robin, Thomas, Vicomte de Coulogne 65, 67, 68
Rondeau, Pierre 45
Rossignol 16, 23
Saint-Étienne de La Tour, Charles 46, 65, 74, 88
Saint-Étienne de La Tour, Claude 46, 65, 88
Sarcel, Sieur de Prévert, Jean 24
Sasinou, Chief 29, 60
Secoudon, Chief 34, 35, 39, 49, 50, 60
Simon, Jean-Jacques 80
Sully, Duc de 59
Theatre of Neptune (*Théâtre de Neptune*) 1, 50, 51
Timothée, Captain 6, 12, 25
Turner, Lieutenant 85
Verrazzano, Giovanni da 6
Vozelles, Pierre 45